FORDSBURG
FIGHTER

Dedication

So many people provided help, hope, companionship
and encouragement to me over the years. I thank them
all and it is to them that this book is dedicated.

FORDSBURG FIGHTER

the journey of an MK volunteer

Amin Cajee

as told to Terry Bell

face2face

First published in 2016 by Face2Face
An imprint of Cover2Cover Books
www.cover2cover.co.za

ISBN: 978-0-9946744-2-5
e-ISBN: 978-1-928346-24-1

Typesetting and book design: Peter Bosman
Editing: Pat Tucker
Proofreading: Clarity Editorial
Printed and bound by Paarl Print, Paarl

COVER IMAGE
R&R in Czechoslovakia: potential MK guerrilla fighters Zelani Mkhonzo (seated) and (from left) Omar Moosa (Bhamjee), Amin Kajee (Cajee) and Joseph Cotton (Kotane), relax in Brno.

PHOTO CREDITS
The image on page 14 is from Philip Bawcombe's *Johannesburg*. Used with permission of his estate.
The photograph on page 16 is used with permission of UWC-Robben Island Museum Mayibuye Archives, Eli Weinberg Collection.
The photograph on page 19 by Eli Weinberg, courtesy of the Don Pinnock archive.
All other photographs were provided by the Cajee family.

Contents

Foreword   vi

Preface   vii

CHAPTER 1   Scared to death   1

CHAPTER 2   Reflections on an early life   10

CHAPTER 3   Pamphlets, slogans and Nelson Mandela   18

CHAPTER 4   Opening blasts of a liberation war   27

CHAPTER 5   And so to Mombasa   37

CHAPTER 6   Journey to the UK   46

CHAPTER 7   Tourists in London   53

CHAPTER 8   Czechoslovakia   62

CHAPTER 9   Getting down to training   69

CHAPTER 10   Cover blown ... and back to Prague   80

CHAPTER 11   At last, Kongwa transit camp   86

CHAPTER 12   Kongwa and the 'people's court'   93

CHAPTER 13   The Czech contingent arrives   103

CHAPTER 14   Swelling biscuits and World War II   109

CHAPTER 15   'In the name of the people' – a death sentence   116

CHAPTER 16   A deadly experiment   122

CHAPTER 17   More corruption ... and worrying news   127

CHAPTER 18   Waiting, planning and getting out   134

CHAPTER 19   Surprise arrivals on the road to Nairobi   139

CHAPTER 20   Name changes and refugee status   145

CHAPTER 21   Zimbabwe, Wankie and looking to Europe   152

CHAPTER 22   A roundabout route to Europe   157

CHAPTER 23   Coming to terms with exile   165

Afterword   176

MK deaths in the Zimbabwe incursions 1967/68   180

Major figures in a seven year odyssey   181

Acknowledgements   183

Notes   184

Foreword

I have known Amin Cajee since 1960. He and his older brother Joe lived just four blocks away from me in Avenue Road, Fordsburg. They showed an interest in the Transvaal Indian Youth Congress's (TIYC) activities, which had a strong following in Fordsburg at the time. Many youth attended TIYC gatherings and demonstrations and gained their political knowledge through these activities.

In 1957 the One Day Strike was held in Johannesburg, the Treason Trial began and the TIYC organised a torch-lit march on Red Square, which was attended by many learners and students. Baton-wielding police officers, accompanied by dogs, attacked demonstrators at this march. In retaliation, participants challenged the police, knocking some of them to the ground. One police officer was so shocked at the response that he was unable to pull out his gun. The talk at the police station the next day was that '... last night the coolies were very cross'. Amin vividly recalls this episode, among many others, in his book.

Amin and his close friends Omar Bhamjee and Magan Narsi became active members of the TIYC, attending demonstrations and helping to print, store and distribute leaflets, put up posters calling for strike action and paint slogans. They were asked to be on the executive committee of the organisation and attended meetings locally and in Johannesburg. Amin and his brother Joe also hosted meetings in their bedroom of the house on Avenue Road. Nelson Mandela attended one such meeting to address a group of activists and Amin's mother and sisters fondly remember his politeness in thanking them for their hospitality. On Mandela's arrest, Amin's mother volunteered to help arrange his meals at the Old Fort.

When Umkhonto we Sizwe ('Spear of the Nation') (MK) was launched in 1961, there was a drive to recruit young people. We had to be selective about who we recruited. At just 19 years old, Amin, along with Omar and Magan, was recruited into an MK cell led by me. We carried out various undercover activities. In 1962 the organisation's regional command asked volunteers to go abroad for specialised training. As head of the cell, I asked Amin and Omar, who readily agreed to become MK soldiers. They left for East Africa on 22 October 1962, travelling by train and boat. They were the first Indian recruits to leave South Africa to join MK in exile. Once they left South Africa, it was no longer our function to keep track of their progress or whereabouts. They became the responsibility of the external African National Congress (ANC)mission abroad. After Amin and Omar left, and unknown to them, I recruited Amin's brother Joe, who joined Magan in my cell.

Amin has told his story of his involvement in the political movement, especially of his time in MK.

What happened to them and to the others in that chaotic and confused time is both sad and tragic. But his honestly told story is an essential one for us to gain a fuller picture of our history, if only to ensure, perhaps, that future generations will learn from our mistakes.

Paul Joseph

Preface

Over the years, and especially since the 1980s, many friends have wanted me to relate my experiences in the movement (the ANC) and to put something on record. They kept telling me it was important. But I thought: 'Important for whom? I am not going to publish it, and what has happened has happened.'

About five years ago Terry Bell threatened that one day he would come to my home and stay for as long as it might take to record my story. He argued that stories of the past were essential to help understand the present and plan for the future. I was not convinced.

Shortly after this conversation, my granddaughter, Zaqiya, aged eight, was asked at school to write a brief note to say who inspired her and she wrote: 'My Grandad. He met Nelson Mandela and he bombed some pylons in South Africa.' Only some of that was, of course, true.

Then my grandson, Yahya, aged six and on our visit in 2012 to the Olympic Village in London, asked his mum why there was so much security. She explained that it was to track down terrorists, and he loudly proclaimed: 'My granddad was not a terrorist. He was a freedom fighter. He was fighting bad people.' His mother quickly told him to shush.

Obviously, over the years, they had heard, in a household such as ours, conversations about aspects of the anti-apartheid struggle in South Africa. Here was my audience, the people I wanted to speak to. So I decided to start writing down some of my memories. That was all I intended to do.

But Terry Bell turned up and, over the next two years, in person or by email, more and more recollections came to the surface.

So it was that I provided him with what he called a 'verbal jigsaw'. I also traced documents that were written in 1968 and rediscovered a box of photographs of me and some of the other MK trainees in Czechoslovakia. We even tracked down some of the few survivors of my time as an MK soldier.

The result is this book. It is much longer and more detailed than when I first thought of it, but I still see it as a story for my grandchildren. In it, I have tried to be as honest as possible because that is what, I think, my grandchildren deserve.

Amin Cajee
London, 2016

CHAPTER I

Sentenced to death

The words echoed in my head: 'You are guilty of high treason and the penalty is death.' I froze. Terrified. It was September 1966; I was 24 years old. I was in Kongwa, an African National Congress (ANC) camp in Tanzania. And I was going to die.

The man who spoke those words was Joe Modise, a senior representative of the ANC, a movement that claimed to represent 'the people of South Africa' – a phrase we were to hear interminably in the years that followed – and which, we were often told, should be regarded as our mother and father. We were all South Africans a long way from home, away from families and friends, frustrated fighters stranded in a foreign country and totally reliant on the ANC. The movement had control over every aspect of our lives.

I had no idea what would happen when my name was called out in the camp and I was escorted into a room to stand before a tribunal. I, and others in the camp, knew that a hearing was about to take place. We thought it was an inquiry into what had happened a week earlier when one group of comrades had launched an attack on others. But it very quickly became clear that this was not the case. As I stood to attention before the tribunal, Joe Modise revealed that they were not interested in the clashes that had taken place, in which I was among the injured.

Looking severe, Joe informed me that I was being charged with high treason. With the help of a foreign power, I and others had plotted to overthrow the leadership of the ANC. The other accused were friends of mine – 'Pat'* (Patrick Molaoa), who had been an accused in South Africa's notorious Treason Trial;[1] 'Mntungwa' (Vincent Khumalo); 'Ali' (Hussain Jacobs); and 'Mogorosi' (Michael Thomolang). They were to be tried separately and the penalty we all faced was death.

I remained mute, staring blankly ahead, my mind racing and unable to make any sense of the charge. The other four panel members – 'Paul Peterson' (Basil February), Boycie Bodibe, Chris Hani and Jack Gatiep – looked on

---

* Most of the volunteers used 'exile names'. These names appear in quotation marks. Where the given names are known, they are included in parentheses.

impassively as Joe informed me that there were witnesses to a meeting at which this plot had been hatched. They had given evidence that we, the accused, had all been in touch with the Chinese embassy in the Tanzanian capital, Dar es Salaam (Dar). It was the Chinese who were to supply the necessary means to achieve our treasonous objective.

This was insane. I blurted out: 'You are not serious, are you?' But they were. They were charging us with having established links with the Chinese embassy, 240km (150 miles) away to the south-east, in Dar, when we were restricted to the immediate area of the camp and village, without postal, let alone radio, communications. And the Chinese government apparently wanted us to take over a South African liberation movement!

Before I could say anything else, Chris emphasised the seriousness of the charge, with Boycie following and threatening me with very serious consequences, among them execution in various brutal ways. I denied that I had been involved in anything treasonous and asked who the witnesses were and if I could question them. The request was refused. The tribunal would neither identify the witnesses nor allow them to be questioned. I was guilty and would have to die. It was then that I was thrown a cynical lifeline by 'Paul Peterson' and the whole vicious, nasty picture fell into place.

'Paul' addressed me in a friendly way, telling me that 'all this can be sorted out'. What I had to do was to confirm that 'Pat' and 'Mntungwa' were the two people who had initiated the scheme. Should I comply, the panel would consider that I had been misled. All I would then have to do would be to apologise and the tribunal would put in a good word with the leadership.

I realised then that the whole charade was really about 'Pat' and 'Mntungwa', who were apparently seen by Joe as a threat to his position as a senior commander at a time when there seemed to be much jockeying for power and position. Both were well known in the movement in South Africa and had considerable support in the camp. Unlike Joe, they had held top positions in the ANC before it was banned and were widely respected. They were also among the earliest recruits to MK when it was decided to embark on an armed struggle and had initially been sent for training in China. But now China and the ANC's main backer, the Soviet Union, were at loggerheads. This, as I was later to discover, was the great Sino-Soviet split.

The Soviet Union had embarked on a policy of peaceful co-existence with the United States and the West, which the Chinese opposed. The South African Communist Party (SACP) supported the 'Moscow line'. What I think none of us, including the SACP members, realised until much later was that this also meant not encouraging a real underground armed struggle and concentrating instead on conventional warfare training. This was the background to the later incursions into Rhodesia (now Zimbabwe) that are known as the Wankie and Sipolilo campaigns, which were the reason for the decision made by some of us to leave MK.

When I refused to agree to what Paul suggested, the panel threatened me with serious consequences. My death sentence, I was told, could mean being taken to a game park where I would be left for wild animals to tear me to bits. I was frightened, but I couldn't help them, and said so. An order was given and I was marched out and locked in a tiny adjoining room that had apparently been designed as a command centre toilet, should plumbing ever arrive, but was then used as a cell. It was windowless and less than two metres long and perhaps half as wide. I was left there for several hours before being marched out again to face the panel.

It was a repeat of what had gone before and I realised that I had been dragged into a bitter power struggle that seemed to be based on language lines – between isiXhosa speakers from the Cape and isiZulu speakers from Natal. There had also been an incident weeks earlier involving 29 members of the 'Natal' group. Although Modise was from Johannesburg and was a Setswana speaker, he had, at that stage, allied himself with members of what was referred to as the 'Cape group'.

The incident that triggered my trial for 'treason' was subsequently referred to as Operation 29 because that was the number of Natal comrades who had mutinied by taking the camp's only truck.

Late one morning at the end of August 1966, I was relaxing in the tent I shared with eight other comrades when I heard my close friend Omar shouting excitedly for me. I rushed out to hear from him that the Natal group had boarded the truck and left the camp at high speed. There was pandemonium, with the camp commanders running around trying to control the situation. At least an hour passed before the camp was calm again and an assembly was called.

Jack Gatiep, one of the commanders, addressed us. He said in a matter-of-fact way that there had been a mutiny by a group of 29 comrades who had taken control of the camp's truck and had absconded. Dar es Salaam had been informed and the Tanzanian liaison official at our camp, Major Chikombele, had alerted the Tanzanian authorities.

But then Jack's language and mood changed. These men who had taken the truck, he said, were traitors and deserters, enemies of 'the people of South

Africa'. The men were members of a group that had been planted by the South African security forces. They would be caught and dealt with without mercy. This rhetoric seemed to inflame the mood of some of the comrades and Chris Hani led the charge, calling for the death penalty when they were caught. Several others called for the offenders to be shot.

Gatiep then announced a curfew and appointed a special platoon which seemed to comprise mainly supporters of the Cape group, to patrol the camp. It would, we were told, shoot on sight anyone suspected of rebelling against the camp administration. This announcement added fuel to the rumour that, although the Tanzanian government had not allowed us to have arms, some of the commanders might, indeed, have guns. What was beyond doubt, however, was that tribal tensions were coming to a head as a result of 'Operation 29'.

When we were finally dismissed, six of us got together to assess the situation. The comrades who had taken the truck were all from Natal and included some of my closest associates, among them Karl and Reggie, along with Rubin, who was the acknowledged leader of the Natal group. Significantly, most of the speeches and denunciations, along with the calls for the death penalty, seemed orchestrated and had come from among the Cape group. But the majority of the comrades were subdued and made no contribution to the debate.

I was disappointed when I realised that Karl, who was such a close comrade, had not confided in me about the action, especially considering that it must have been planned way ahead of time. But I also realised that it had been in my best interests that I knew nothing about what was planned and that I was not involved in any way.

As we heard later, the Tanzanian army set up a roadblock near Morogoro, on the road south to Zambia and South Africa. The truck was intercepted and the comrades were returned, under escort, to Kongwa. It was about 4pm when the truck trundled into camp, with the comrades in the back in high spirits, singing freedom songs. The camp commanders seemed to be taken by surprise and obviously did not know how to respond to their arrival. The 29 disembarked, formed ranks and stood to attention, waiting for instructions from the commanders. The rest of us stood around watching the spectacle. Some of the onlookers were evidently amused, others were angry and most seemed indifferent to what was going on.

Rubin stepped forward from the ranks of the Natal group and addressed the commanders and the rest of us. The reason for taking the vehicle, he said, was in order to convey the grievances of the comrades in Kongwa to the leadership in Lusaka. For years there had been no serious attempt to move the struggle south and into South Africa. What they had done was to highlight their frustration at the inaction of the leadership. They now hoped that the leadership would take their demands seriously and move the struggle forward.

The commanders, having bayed for the blood of the 'traitors and deserters', were at a loss as to how to handle the situation. Eventually, they simply dismissed the group after telling them it was not the end of the matter; the 29 would be tried for mutiny. One person present who was obviously amused was Major Chikombele.

As we waited for the next move from the commanders, the atmosphere in the camp was extremely tense. Groups were coalescing and Jack Gatiep; 'Zola Zembe' (Archie Sibeko), who had also been a 1956 Treason Trialist; and Chris and Paul, who were senior figures in both the Cape group and the camp, were seen meeting at different locations late into the night. Not being part of the major groups identified either with the Cape or Natal, my friend Omar and I kept a low profile. At this point Karl sent a message for us to keep away. Something was bound to happen, but I think most of us hoped that the episode with the truck would galvanise the leadership into action and that we would soon be moving south.

As we hoped, it was only a matter of days before some of the top leadership arrived in Kongwa. Acting ANC president Oliver Tambo (known as OR – his second name was Reginald) came along with leading ANC and SACP leaders Moses Kotane, JB Marks and Moses Mabhida, a major ANC figure in Natal. With them were Mzwai Philiso, Mendi Msimang and Joe Modise.

Meetings were held with the commanders, but JB Marks also made a point of talking with the rank and file. We had some frank discussions and he was very attentive, asking questions and inviting suggestions. He wanted to know when and where things had started going wrong. We felt comfortable sitting and talking with him: he was easygoing and approachable. Moses Mabhida went into conclave with the rebellious Natal group, but the other leaders restricted themselves to discussions with the camp commanders.

After two days of these talks an assembly was called. Oliver Tambo stood up to address us, and what he said took us completely by surprise. He did not mention any of the issues that had resulted in the so-called mutiny – issues like the poor conditions in the camp, the low morale and the frustration at being kept in limbo. Instead, he launched a scathing attack on the group that had taken the truck. He said a panel of judges had been selected to try the group for mutiny and they would be judged and sentenced accordingly. He added that what had happened was a serious crime against the people of South Africa and could not go unpunished.

Tambo concluded that he had other important business to attend to and was leaving with the rest of the leadership for Dar es Salaam. However, we noticed that Moses Mabhida did not leave. He stayed behind for the trial, which was scheduled for the following day. It would be held in the dining hall, a large building that had been erected by comrades in 1965 and was a great improvement on having to eat in the open, usually under the scorching sun, or in our tents when it rained. The hall was sparsely furnished, the few tables and chairs made by comrades who were carpenters and had managed to obtain some timber. Mostly, we sat on the floor.

On the morning of the trial 'Pat', 'Mntungwa', 'Ali', 'Mogorosi' and I sat a distance from the dining hall and observed the comings and goings at the far end of the camp, near what we called the armoury, which was, in fact, where our store of uniforms and other equipment were kept, but contained no weapons. A quite large group from the Cape assembled nearby and were in deep discussion; the rest of the comrades were spread around the camp, either on their own or in small groups. The atmosphere was not particularly tense.

After some time an assembly was called. We formed up and were marched into the hall. There were more than 400 of us in Kongwa then and we crammed into every available space, leaving room at the front where there was a table and four chairs for the panel of judges. The 29 'mutineers' took their place to the right of the area reserved for the panel. While we waited, some of us noticed that Mabhida had seated himself in the middle of the hall. Our small group, which included 'Pat', 'Mntungwa', 'Ali' and Omar, and which was not aligned to either of the factions, sat together to the left of the hall.

When the judges entered we noted that all of them, with the exception of Joe Modise, who took the chair, were isiXhosa speakers from the Cape: Chris Hani, 'Paul Peterson', Jack Gatieb and 'Zola Zembe'. The accused sat to the right of the panel, facing the assembly. This was to be an open court and all were free to speak. Modise, in his opening statement, repeated Tambo's words, but stressed that the assembled comrades would be given the opportunity to have their say.

So began what looked like the beginnings of a tragi-comedy as apparently handpicked members, particularly from the Cape, were called on to make contributions. In each case these comrades expressed outrage and demanded the death penalty, suggesting that the 'mutineers' be either shot or hanged. After two hours, as lunchtime approached, the hearing was adjourned.

During the lunch break a group of us discussed the morning's proceedings and decided that we had to make our voices heard. We could not allow what was a show trial choreographed by Joe Modise to go unchallenged. We knew that a large number of comrades, clearly the majority, sympathised with what the Natal group had done, even if they were too intimidated to say so publicly. What we needed was to change the mood and this we could do by speaking out.

When we reassembled we fully expected to be denied our right to be heard, especially when Joe asked if there was any other contribution to the trial before he asked the leader of the Natal group, Rubin, to speak. 'Pat' raised his hand and there was total silence as Joe did not react. But then Moses Mabhida signalled to the panel that 'Pat' wanted to speak and Joe had no option but to give him permission.

That broke the silence and one speaker after another stood up to state that what the Natal group had done was to highlight not only the frustration we all felt, but also the many broken promises of the leadership about moving south. The deterioration in the health of a number of comrades as a result of poor diet and the lack of medical facilities and supplies also featured prominently, as did criticism of the lack of accountability on the part of the commanders. Comrades pointed out that they had felt for a long time that it was better to fight and die in South Africa than to rot in a country thousands of miles away.

Even those speakers who conceded that the manner in which the protest had been carried out was not right, noted that they saw no other option because there was no access to leaders, who rarely appeared and who seemed to ignore the concerns of the rank and file. It was hoped that the desired effect of the protest would be achieved and that the leadership would heed the demands of the majority of the comrades to move south.

Everyone who spoke on this basis also emphasised how history would record the killing of a group of freedom fighters from Natal by the ANC when their only crime was to have put pressure on the leadership to return to South Africa to fight. Throughout, great care was taken not to inflame the situation by mentioning any ethnic or linguistic tensions. In any event, there were also a number of obviously disenchanted comrades in the Cape group.

Finally, it was Rubin's turn to speak. By that time it was obvious that the Natal group had the support of the majority. Judging by the scowls and the body language, this did not go down well with Joe and the panel. In his closing remarks, Joe accused those of us who had spoken out of being 'self-styled lawyers' who were in league with groups opposed to the leadership of the ANC and the people of South Africa. He was getting into his stride when Moses Mabhida raised his hand to speak. He could not be denied.

The softly-spoken SACP leader offered only mild criticism of the action of the Natal group. At the same time, he acknowledged the frustration not only of the group but of other members of the ANC army at the delay in moving south. He noted that the panel of judges had to be mindful about the punishment they intended to give and the grave consequences if they decided to overstep their authority.

Mabhida was probably aware that deep ethnic – tribal – feelings had taken root some time before and that the command structure within the camp had exacerbated these. We knew that Joe's close relationship at the time with the Cape group was a matter of convenience – earlier he had been on the same sort of terms with 'Pat' and had complained that the tribal element in the ANC favoured the Xhosas.

Two and a half hours later the panel retired to the offices in the armoury building to consider the evidence. For the next hour or so we all observed frequent comings and goings between the tent to which Moses Mabhida had retreated and the armoury before the panel finally emerged, followed by Mabhida. We were called to assemble and marched back into the hall.

Our little group was pleased with the way things had gone and were certain no extreme punishments would be meted out. Mabhida, as the most senior leader at the trial, had clearly not favoured harsh measures and had probably instructed the panel about what sentence would be appropriate. So it turned out, although we were surprised at the leniency when the sentence was announced: the accused were effectively confined to barracks – confined within the perimeter of the camp – for two weeks. Morale seemed to soar and I think we all thought things were about to change gear and we would be heading south to start the liberation war.

It was not to be. A week after the trial, at around ten in the morning, I was sitting in my tent when I heard shouts and a clatter of activity outside. As I stepped out of the tent flap I saw about five groups, each comprising about three or four men, brandishing sticks and knives, running from tent to tent and attacking other comrades. The focus of the attacks, which seemed to be led by 'Zembe', were the tents accommodating the Natal comrades. I was joined by Omar and 'Mntungwa' and we were moving away from the area when we were accosted by comrades armed with knives and sticks. The attack was merciless and all I remember was blocking everything they threw at us with my arms. When another group intervened on our side, the attackers fled.

I was bleeding from my head and nose where the sticks had landed and there was a stab wound in the palm of my hand, the result of a blocked knife attack. Victor helped me to the clinic and I could see Ali struggling from the beating, but not bleeding. 'Mntungwa' was being carried, bleeding heavily as he had been stabbed in a number of places. He was clearly the main target of the attack and was hospitalised. I had ten stitches to my head and several to my palm.

Rachel, one of the two nurses in the camp, attended to me while screaming at the people who had attacked us. Victor and Albert also remonstrated with them. Everybody had been caught unawares by the attack, but the Natal group quickly mobilised and, heavily armed with sticks, pangas and knives, created a defence line.

Word reached Major Chikombele, who came and spoke to us in the clinic. He was visibly upset and said he would take the camp commanders to task for allowing the attack. I was still in the clinic when I heard that the Natal group had repulsed the main attack and very few of them had been beaten up or had suffered any injuries. I also heard that 'Pat' had avoided the whole fracas. He, presumably another major target, was far away at the toilets when the attack took place. By the time he arrived on the scene everything was over.

The next morning Joe Modise returned to a camp riddled with paranoia and fear and consisting of heavily armed factions. With his return came the announcement that another tribunal had been set up. And this was the occasion on which I was sentenced to death – and offered a reprieve, but only if I would effectively confirm a similar sentence on good friends and comrades.

CHAPTER 2

Reflections on an early life

It is said that when you fear you are about to die your life flashes before you. I don't know about that. What I do know is that I thought it very possible, as I sat in that cell, that I would die within the next 24 or 48 hours. And my whole life paraded slowly and clearly through my memory. Reviewing the past was probably the best way to avoid thinking about the future.

Even now, thinking back, it was probably inevitable that I would have rebelled against the system into which I was born. Probably equally inevitable was that I would join a movement that seemed to embody all the hopes I held for the future.

I was born on 24 September 1942 into relative poverty in the town of Middelburg in what was then the Transvaal province of South Africa, the youngest of nine children. My parents had migrated in about 1930 to South Africa from a small village in the state of Gujarat in India and had eventually set up a small corner shop in Middelburg, where they sold sweets, fruit and soft drinks. From vague memories and from what I subsequently heard, it was a hand-to-mouth existence, but my father managed to keep his head above the waters of ever-present debt.

Then, as World War II came to an end, there were disturbing political developments. The overtly racist Herenigde Nasionale Party and the Afrikaner Party, which had formed a coalition, were making much of the running, especially in the rural areas and small towns such as Middelburg. And a particular campaign of these parties was the repatriation not only of Indian migrants, but also of people of Indian descent who were born in the country or whose families had been in South Africa for two or three generations.

There were undoubtedly many people of Indian descent – and especially more recent migrants – who must have been deeply concerned about these developments. It could have been this that drove my father, in 1947, to travel back to India, perhaps to see if there was a safe haven for us should things go badly wrong in South Africa. Whatever the reason, he was in India when the Herenigde Nasionale Party came into power in 1948 – and promptly halted all migration from India. This included South Africans of Indian origin who were visiting India at the time. As formal apartheid and *blanke baasskap* (white domination) kicked in, the only immigration that would be encouraged was that from Europe.

I recall that there were many representations over the years to try to get my father back, but to no avail. Initially this left my mother to try to hold the family and the business together. My two oldest brothers, who were in their twenties, tried to manage the shop, our only source of income. But they lacked the experience of my father and perhaps trading conditions had worsened. Whatever the reason, the shop closed and the family moved to Johannesburg, where I began my schooling at the Bree Street Primary School, which catered for children from the rather run-down, overcrowded and vibrant inner city Indian ghetto of Fordsburg.

I have no idea how my mother managed, but, by 1950, when my older brothers married and moved on, she found herself in financial difficulties. There were still seven children at home – my four sisters, me and my brothers Yussuf (often called Joe) and Bashir. My mother was aware that there was an institution, the Waterval Islamic Institute, a boarding school for indigent Muslim children, north of Johannesburg. It was known as Mia's Farm. The girls' hostel was about a mile from the accommodation provided for boys and it was to this place that my mother sent my brother Joe, my sister Jamila and me. We had very few clothes and no money, but the place at least provided us with a roof over our heads and three meals a day. The three of us returned only for school holidays, when my mother had somehow saved up enough money to feed us and our four siblings.

The holidays were a relief, because Mia's Farm was a place of horrors. The discipline was harsh and the routine rigid. The wake-up call came at 5.30am every morning to attend prayers and study the Quran. Then it was breakfast at 7am, with school starting an hour later, followed by prayers at 1pm, lunch at 1.30pm and back to school until 2.30pm. From 3pm to 5pm there was Islamic studies followed by a one-hour break, during which we could play soccer and cricket or just laze around before prayers and supper at 7pm. We had prayers at 8pm and went to our rooms by 8.30pm for lights out.

There were about 20 rooms, with about 25 students to a room, and the disciplinary regime was strict to the point of physical abuse. When you committed any violation of the rules, however minor, you were offered a choice of six of the best or the 'machine gun'. Six of the best was when the teacher, wielding a cane lifted behind his shoulder, brought it down hard, six times, on the buttocks. The machine gun required you being held down by two boys while the cane, held a short distance from, and level with, your behind was used to mount a rapid attack on your buttocks that sounded like a machine gun.

Another punishment required the victim to squat with his hands behind his knees while grabbing hold of both ears. In this extremely awkward position he then had to make his way from one end of the room to the other. Often, while a student was in this squatting position and moving with difficulty, the tutor would kick the victim, who would go rolling over head first, knocking into the desks. There was also an especially sadistic punishment during the Islamic classes. When any of us failed to give a correct answer to a question the tutor would call us up individually and put his hand into one pocket of our trousers, reach across and squeeze our testicles; the pain was excruciating.

But, in many ways, these punishments paled into insignificance against the humiliation of being sent to sleep in the 'pee pot room'. This was a room set aside for boys who wet their beds. There was no attempt to find out why this happened. Anyone guilty of doing so – and that included boys of all ages – was sent to this room. The prospect terrified us, because, despite being humiliating, the stench of urine in the room was almost unbearable. No attempt was ever made to clean it up.

Given these circumstances, it is little wonder that I wanted desperately to leave. I still have a very clear memory of my sister and me just walking out of the institute one day. We spun some story that enabled us to get onto a bus without paying and to get to the station in Johannesburg. From there, we walked the remaining 1.5km or so to our home in the largely Indian area of Fordsburg. My mother and sisters heard us out and my mother promised that arrangements would be made for us to come home soon for good. But we could not be allowed to stay at home then. By 5pm that day, we were back at the institute and waiting for our punishment. But when my name was called, Joe stepped out and took my caning. My sister escaped unpunished because she was a girl and different conditions applied.

After some time there was a slight improvement in the family's financial position and my mother felt she could support us at home. But when she approached the authorities at Mia's Farm they refused to release us, on the grounds that we had been given up to the institute to be trained in Islamic studies. Our mother must have been distraught. She had come from India and did not speak English, although she was well versed in both spoken and written Urdu and Gujarati. I mention this because I, and many like me at the time, considered people who did not speak English to be illiterate. The Mias took advantage of my mother's lack of English to deny her the return of her children.

However, she was determined to get us back and went around making enquiries. Through a friend, she was put in touch with a German woman of Jewish origin called Mrs Katz, a social worker who was well known in the Indian community. Mrs Katz did exceptional work assisting people in need of food and medical and social care and taking on the apartheid authorities when necessary.

On behalf of my mother, Mrs Katz investigated the institute's claim to us and, in the process, discovered that Mia's Farm was given financial assistance by the government to provide for orphans and the homeless during holidays. It appeared that money was collected on our behalf on the basis that we did not have a home to go to. But we not only did have a home, we went there every holiday. When it was pointed out to the officials at the institute that they were making fraudulent welfare claims, we were released immediately to our, by then, very overcrowded family home.

It was 1952 and the wife of one of my older brothers had died, so he and his two children, Feroz, aged two, and six-month-old Naeem, had moved into the two-bedroomed house. It was quite a squash, but it gave my mother some financial stability because my brother was contributing to the household finances. It was still a difficult time and it was perhaps for financial reasons that the family moved to Roodepoort, west of Johannesburg, for a year before coming back to Fordsburg in 1954, to much improved living conditions, with extra bedrooms and even a separate dining room.

Although my schooling had been disrupted, I went back to the Bree Street Primary School, where I completed my final year and looked forward to graduating to the nearby high school. At that stage I think I was blissfully unaware that I had suffered any disadvantage educationally or, indeed, in any other way, but a rude awakening jolted me into political awareness and set me on my journey to a prison cell in Tanzania.

The awakening came when I entered high school in 1955 and the Group Areas Act of 1950 was applied to Fordsburg. This act gave the government the power to create designated areas for what it termed 'Europeans' and 'non-Europeans' and, in 1955, it was decreed that all people classified as 'Indian' and living in inner city areas such as Fordsburg should be relocated to a designated area known as Lenasia, which lay some 32km to the southwest in what was then open countryside.

Fordsburg, where the young Amin went to school and began his political life, has a history of radical political activity. It's also the home to many historical buildings. This one, Sachs Hotel (still standing on the corner of Central Avenue and Main Road) is one of several that caught fire during the 1922 Miners' Strike. This characterful sketch was done in the early 1970s by watercolourist Philip Bawcombe.

The government argued, as it did for the demolition of the whole inner city suburb of District Six in Cape Town in 1966, that Fordsburg was a slum. This was by no means the truth, although many of the buildings were somewhat ramshackle and shabby and the area was overcrowded, a situation caused by apartheid laws that confined 'Indians' to the one area. Disparate, often fractious, it was a vibrant suburb close to the city where doctors and accountants, layabouts, manual workers, waiters, businessmen and crooks lived side by side.

Most of the community resisted the move, but they protested and petitioned to no avail. The government, obviously fearful of an international outcry should forced removals be carried out, decided to apply pressure. And where better than with schooling. All Fordsburg schools, which were state schools, were simply closed down and relocated to Lenasia. This meant that the children of families who refused to move had to undertake a daily 64km round trip. The increased cost, especially for poorer families, often proved crippling, and there were also concerns about the safety of children travelling on their own.

The government had created a nightmare for families who dared to resist.

The only secondary (high) school in the area was also closed down at the end of 1954 and the government set up several prefabricated classrooms in Lenasia, staffed by 12 teachers. When the new school year started the teachers had very little to do, as the majority of the Fordsburg community boycotted the move. This was what alerted me and many of my contemporaries to the realities of South Africa at the time. Until then, many of us had not been fully aware that there were four classes of citizen: in the first class were those classified 'white' or 'European'; the second class – and a long way down from first – were the 'coloureds', people of 'mixed' parentage; followed closely by the 'Indians' or 'Asiatics'; and then, very much at the bottom of the pile, the 'black' African majority.

Awareness of this reality was encouraged by an alternative school that was established at that time in Fordsburg. But it was an alternative that some parents were afraid to support openly for fear of victimisation by the security police.

The school was known as Central Indian High School (CIHS) and when it opened its doors 400 students enrolled. It had been established by the Indian Congress, which had been founded by Mahatma Gandhi in 1894 and which had formed an alliance with the ANC, the Coloured People's Congress and the white Congress of Democrats (COD). Funded by contributions from the community and from whatever fees the families of students could pay, it had as its first principal a 'listed communist',[2] Michael Harmel. The Afrikaans language teacher was Molly Fischer, activist wife of Bram Fischer, an advocate who was, in 1965, sentenced to life imprisonment for his anti-apartheid activities and his membership of the underground SACP.

My older brother Joe and his age group were the first to be affected by the school closures, and attended CIHS. It was Joe who made me aware of the nature of apartheid and the many issues that affected us. By the time I got to CIHS it had changed premises three times, as the government put pressure on landlords to terminate every lease. As a result, the school committee was almost always on the lookout for new premises.

In my first year as a CIHS student we moved premises twice and were finally located at the local mosque, which had four classrooms that were used for religious lessons in the afternoons, so the school occupied the rooms in the mornings. But there was not enough accommodation since CIHS's policy was that nobody should be turned away. At the same time there was a huge influx of students, as resistance to the Group Areas removals grew.

Teachers at Fordsburg's Central Indian High School included some of the best known names in the anti-apartheid movement, among them (from left to right): Mervyn Thandary, Alfred Hutchinson, Duma Nokwe, Michael Harmel, Moosajee and (front) Molly Fischer and Joan Anderson.

I recall that for the first two months I was at CIHS there were about 100 students in each class, three to a desk. I and two other students used to sit on a windowsill.

To improve the situation the classes were split in two – one indoors, the other outside on the lawn. Classes took turns in the two areas, changing over in mid-morning. Sitting outside had its own problems – hot in summer and cold in winter. And then, of course, there was the rain, when 'outsiders' all had to dash indoors. But the situation did improve when what used to be residential homes around the corner became vacant, probably as a result of families relocating to Lenasia, and we were provided with six additional classrooms.

The school was the only one in the country to be staffed by a real representation of the citizens of South Africa. The teachers were drawn from what the government classified as the African, Indian, coloured and white groups. This was, in itself, unique at the time. But it was unique in other ways too: most of the staff were actively involved in anti-apartheid politics. The staff list read like a who's who of the Congress movement. Along with Michael

Harmel and Molly Fischer, there were many other activists, including Duma Nokwe, who would become secretary-general of the ANC.[3] Can Themba, best known as a journalist and novelist, also taught at CIHS.

Having these teachers had certain drawbacks, through no fault of their own. The school was regularly raided by the Special Branch on the pretext that we were being taught revolution. Our history notes on the French Revolution were confiscated and many of our teachers were arrested from time to time. This harassment may have interrupted our education, but it always strengthened our resolve.

There were times when our teachers taught us without being paid for up to three months and we would have a drive to raise funds through various functions, screening films, and asking for donations. The fees we paid were not sufficient to pay the teachers and many students, including me, defaulted because our families could not afford to pay. Although we were never sent home, it made me uncomfortable to be in this position. What I realise now is the great debt I owe to the teachers, who sacrificed their time and energies to provide us with an education.

Eventually, the constant harassment and the banning and jailing of teachers made the running of the school impossible and control was handed over to a non-political committee of elders. Many of the teachers came from non-political backgrounds and the focus moved away from the Indian Congress. As a result, we had continuity and were free from police harassment. However, it was the experience of my years at the 'Congress school' that I think had the most profound influence on my political development and strengthened my resolve to make a contribution to the struggle for liberation.

CHAPTER 3

Pamphlets, slogans and Nelson Mandela

As I sat hunched in that 'cell' in Tanzania I wondered at how idealistic – and naive – we had been when we set out to join the liberation struggle. It would have been difficult to have been otherwise since we had nothing other than our own political experience to go by, and that experience was limited and coloured by dreams, hopes and faith in a movement and its leadership. We saw ourselves as fighters, as volunteers in an obviously just cause, led by heroes.

I vividly recalled my political awakening following my first involvement in a protest. It was 1959, I was 17 years old, the Treason Trial was in progress and the ANC had called for a one-day 'Stay at Home' protest against a law being considered by the government to prohibit political gatherings. All workers and students were requested to 'stay at home', since a strike would have been illegal. It was a huge success, as workers stayed away from work and we boycotted school.

That evening a torchlight meeting and march was called in the centre of Fordsburg, known as Red Square. Hundreds of men, women and children, many holding homemade torches and candles, gathered in the square, singing freedom songs. On my way to the meeting I had noticed a large number of police vehicles in the surrounding streets. It didn't seem unusual, but what followed was an unexpected and terrifying experience.

About five minutes before we were set to march away from the square, I saw a line of baton-wielding policemen approaching from three differ-ent directions, beating everyone in sight. The crowd, including me, rushed towards the only area on the square free of police. It was at a point where the square was not level with the road and there was a drop of more than a metre to street level. I and some of the younger boys and girls jumped down and assisted other fleeing people as they stumbled over the drop. Then a couple of policemen, obviously unaware of the drop, landed at our feet. We grabbed their batons and frantically beat them before running off as more policemen appeared.

It was chaotic and we were amazed when people in the neighbourhood who had not been on the square, and perhaps didn't even support the march, opened their doors to allow us to escape by running through the houses

TREASON TRIAL

The ACCUSED

DECEMBER 1956

The 1956 Treason Trial accused who later crossed the path of Amin Cajee:
2nd row (from bottom), no. 1: Alfred Hutchinson (teacher at Central Indian
High School); no. 4: Paul Joseph (MK recruiter); no. 6: Moses Kotane (exiled
ANC/SACP leader); no. 8: Ahmed Kathrada (political lecturer); 3rd row,
no. 9: Nelson Rolihlahla Mandela; 4th row, no. 3: Patrick Molaoa (Kongwa
camp comrade & friend); 5th row, no. 7: Duma Nokwe (exiled ANC leader);
7th row, no. 1: OR Tambo (ANC acting president); 8th row, no. 7: Archie –
'Zola Zembe' – Sibeko (Kongwa camp commander); 11th row, no. 6:
Dr Wilson Zamindlela Conco (Luthuli Foundation, London).

and out of the back doors into the yards beyond. It was supposed to be a peaceful demonstration, but many people were badly beaten. Politically, my eyes were starting to open, although it would be another year or so before I, along with my three closest friends, Omar, Magan (Mugs) and Abdul Samad (Blondie), became fully involved in the struggle.

By then Omar and Mugs were working and Blondie and I were still at CIHS. I was also a part-time assistant in the local library, working with Moosa Moosajee, a teacher at the school who was a leading figure in the Indian Congress. It was at the library that I came into contact with a number of active members of the Congress and its youth wing. As a result, our little group started distributing anti-apartheid leaflets, printed locally by printers who supported the movement.

It was fairly low-level political activity, but we also painted slogans on government buildings and prominent walls, demanding such things as freedom, equal pay and 'No to the pass laws' that affected the lives of our ANC comrades. We were young and enthusiastic and I don't think we really considered the danger we were courting. But when, after the 1960 Sharpeville massacre,[4] the government banned the ANC and the Pan Africanist Congress (PAC) and detained, jailed and tortured opponents, we wanted to show that resistance was still alive.

At times we operated in pairs, sometimes with white female colleagues, going into white areas and spraying slogans onto the walls of buildings, aware that if we were caught the police might use the Immorality Act,[5] with its seven-year prison term, to prosecute us. The pass laws, which compelled all Africans to carry a reference book, known as a pass book or dompas, limited the African comrades from working with us, and the curfew laws excluded them, without special permission, from all designated white areas after 10pm. Because we were slightly higher up the apartheid scale this restriction did not apply to us.

At the same time, we worked very hard to try to engage our own community in campaigns as we sought support for strikes and encouraged offers of material and moral support. A number of the better-off families, some of whom owned large businesses, were hostile, but many were supportive, at least in providing material support. Socially, there were class – and sometimes caste – divisions in the community, but all of us, as 'Indians', suffered discrimination, although some a little less than others.

Our leafleting and slogan-painting activities were illegal and therefore carried out clandestinely so as not to attract attention from the security police. And even when we attended demonstrations, it was with other people, many of whom were not involved at any other level. We were effectively underground and, in due course, we were co-opted onto the national executive of the Indian Youth Congress. Even this was done in secret. Times had changed and we no longer held annual elective conferences. So it was that my appointment as joint treasurer (with Shiresh Nanabhai, who later served 11 years on Robben Island) was confirmed at a secret session of the executive committee.

Fordsburg library was the centre for our operations. There we wrote and stored leaflets, held late-night meetings and met and recruited members to congress. It was often frightening and frustrating, but it was also an exciting time, although my mother was not pleased with my involvement and that of my older brother Joe.

She understood why there was a struggle, but she was concerned for our safety and the thought of us being imprisoned caused her a lot of stress. But she never mentioned her concerns, although we were always aware of them. Whenever we were out late at night, for example, we would return to see her standing on the balcony waiting for us, even at 4am. Only when she saw that we were safe, would she go to bed.

Our constant desire was to make a major symbolic impact. We once tried to set off a massive bonfire with used vehicle tyres and petrol, collecting a great many tyres and transporting them in a borrowed car to the base of a nearby mine dump, a great hill of yellow sand deposited by the workings of a gold mine, intending to take them up the mine dump and light them there. But on the night we found it impossible to carry all the tyres to the top. It was still a significant blaze, but hardly what we had intended.

So much effort went into so many of our schemes. For example, for the first anniversary of the massacre at Sharpeville, on 21 March 1961, Costa Gazidis, a young doctor friend and member of the COD, decided we should hoist the ANC flag atop one of the highest office buildings in Braamfontein overlooking the Johannesburg city centre. It should be big enough to be seen from all over the city. Since the ANC and the PAC had been banned in the previous year, we thought this would be an excellent way to show that resistance continued. But we needed a very big flag. This was solved by getting one of my sisters, a dressmaker, to stitch the huge black, green and gold emblem. After all the effort of making it and getting it up at night, it flew for a very short while in the early morning before being hauled down.

*Paul Joseph, the former Treason Trialist who recruited Amin at least twice –
first to work with radical journalist Ruth First in the offices of the* New Age
newspaper in 1961, and later that year, to MK, the ANC's armed wing.

By the time of the flag episode I had completed my schooling and had been
recruited by a former Treason Trialist and congress member, Paul Joseph, to
work briefly with the radical journalist Ruth First in the offices of the *New
Age* newspaper. There I handled the filing and clerical work. This campaign-
ing, Congress-supporting newspaper was sold on the streets by volunteers,
some of whom, like Paul Joseph and Mosie Moola, would compete to see
who could sell the most copies. It was only much later that I discovered that
New Age was, in fact, the mouthpiece of the Communist Party.

In those early days we did not make any distinctions politically. It was a
simple matter of being for or against apartheid. We were anti-apartheid. And
we supported the Congress Alliance and were not even aware that there was
a communist party. What united us was the Freedom Charter, which declared
that South Africa belonged to all who lived in it and that wealth should be
shared and people permitted to work, live and travel where they wished.

But there were inevitable squabbles, often of a personal nature, and there
were lessons to be learned. One of the people who gave me the most help was
Suliman 'Babla' Saloojee. We worked together on a number of anti-government
activities and I learned a crucial lesson from him. On one occasion we had a

disagreement about an activity that we were involved in – I felt that he had put us in a difficult situation, especially had we been caught. Over several weeks I avoided him and refused to speak to him, but one evening he came over to see me. He pointed out that I should remember that in my lifetime I would be confronted with similar situations of disagreement many times over. As a comrade I should treat a difference of opinion on one issue as just that – and move on. To do so would make me a better person and enable me to deal with more important matters in whatever future area of work I might be involved in.

I never forgot that lesson from a man who, I was later to hear, died a horrible death at the hands of the Special Branch. Most of his fingernails were found to be missing when his battered body was examined. He had 'fallen' from the seventh floor interrogation room of the security police headquarters in Johannesburg, known as The Greys. Years later I discovered that he had also not given the police any information, so saving my brother Joe and Terry Bell, who had been working with him to produce a radical publication, *Combat*.

In the early years of my exile I heard from time to time about people I had met who had stayed in the country and the sacrifices they had made. Walter Sisulu, a Rivonia Trialist,[6] spent 25 years in prison and Imam Haroon from the Cape died at the hands of the Special Branch. But such horrors were still to come when the annual general meeting of the Indian Congress was held in 1961. It was decided in advance not to name the new members of the national executive in public. However, well-known figures, known to the police as long-serving members of the executive, would be announced as having been elected.

But playing this name game can have unforeseen consequences. I was at a gathering that the police had declared to be illegal and where they took the names of all those who attended, including mine. In the wake of the gathering the police raided the homes of all those whose names they had. And so it was that a well-known political activist who was much older than me, but who shared the same name, ended up serving a prison term on my behalf. Doha (old man), as I used fondly to call the older Amin Cajee, wasn't even at the gathering, and he never ceased to remind me of the sacrifice he had made for me.

As members of the executive we were instructed to attend monthly meetings. These were held at the homes of a number of individuals, including those of my family. We had a two-bedroom, self-contained flat on the fifth floor of a building in Avenue Road in Fordsburg. There was no lift and, in the early years when I returned from school, I used to fling my school bag from level to level until I reached the fifth floor. The advantage Joe and I had in sharing a bedroom was that it was completely separated from the main apartment. This gave us the freedom to move in and out without the knowledge of our mother and four sisters.

At these meetings we discussed various campaigns that were mounted across the country and allocated tasks to individuals or groups in the executive. At this point it was mainly leaflet distribution, slogan painting and recruiting new members into the movement. We also had speakers from kindred organisations – the ANC; the Indian Congress, parent body of the youth wing; the COD; the Coloured People's Congress and the South African Congress of Trade Unions (SACTU). All the speakers would talk of how they expected various campaigns to progress and enhance the struggle. By 1961 a number of these speakers had gone underground, were banned or were sought by the police and they risked their personal safety to address us.

At one of these meetings in 1961, besides the usual executive, a large number of invited comrades arrived at the family flat. There were three beds in the room, the spare one to accommodate guests, and during our meetings we sat on these beds or on the floor. On this occasion there wasn't even much floor space left and it was obvious some important announcement was going to be made.

There was a considerable air of excitement as we sat chatting among ourselves. But there was sudden silence as there was a knock at the door. It was Babla Saloojee. He looked cautiously into the room before opening the door wider and stepping aside to allow his companion to enter: the companion was Nelson Mandela, the man the media had dubbed the 'Black Pimpernel'. We looked up to him as one of the major leaders, known to us all as Comrade Nelson, and at the time he was underground and on the run, sought everywhere by the police.

His appearance took everybody by surprise and there was a moment of shocked and amazed silence before loud applause erupted. Babla quickly motioned everybody to be silent. It was unnecessary to point out that Nelson Mandela had taken a huge risk in attending this gathering and we quickly deployed people to keep watch outside while the meeting was in progress.

I moved off the bed, gave Comrade Nelson my place, and sat at his feet. He started by saying he was very proud to be present and on behalf of the movement wanted to convey his gratitude to all of us who had been contributing to the struggle for a free South Africa. He went on to give brief details about a trip he had made abroad and his meetings with a number of heads of state. Internationally, he said, we had a lot of support and the national co-ordinating committee was busy drawing up strategies to further the struggle. But he made no reference to any move away from a campaign of passive resistance to armed struggle, a topic that often arose in our meetings. We would also question guest speakers about this and were always told that the time was not right.

So we addressed the issue with the 'Black Pimpernel'. He explained that South Africa was unique in that the army comprised only whites and our black policemen were not armed. Experience in other countries, like Algeria, established a foundation for an armed insurgency because the colonial powers had recruited the local population into their armed forces and had armed the local police. In our case, one option was to send people abroad for military training. The immediate countries along the border with South Africa were not suitable, so it would have to be further north. However, the logistics involved in such a major task needed time and resources. This option needed years of planning; however, it was under discussion.

After two hours the meeting ended, but before Mandela left he asked to meet the head of the household and I took him into the main flat to meet my mother and sisters. He took my mother's hand and thanked her for the refreshments and the hospitality. Saloojee, Indres Naidoo and Shiresh Nanubhai (the latter two later served many years on Robben Island) escorted him out. My mother was very impressed, and when Mandela was arrested later that year, she prayed for him and, while he was held at the Johannesburg Fort prison, prepared meals that were delivered to him.

It seemed amazing, with the police scouring the country looking for him, that Nelson Mandela must have been hiding out in the Fordsburg area. On one Saturday afternoon I almost blundered into what I later realised was a clandestine interview he was giving to a journalist. I had gone to visit two of my friends and comrades, Rams and Nuns, at the Nanubhai family's flats in Lovers' Walk. There were two flats – one for the female members of the family, the parents and the married brother and children, the other for the boys – the two younger brothers and Shiresh. We used this flat for meeting and socialising.

On this particular afternoon Nuns and I walked up to the flat and he opened the door to let me in as he went across to his parents' flat next door.

As I entered the room I became aware of sounds of hurried movement and noticed that there seemed to be people hiding behind a large curtain. I immediately walked out and slammed the door behind me to indicate that I had left. When Nuns returned I mentioned to him that some important meeting must be taking place inside the flat. So we both quickly left the building.

I gave very little thought to this episode as such meetings were far from unusual in those days. But the next morning I picked up a Sunday newspaper and there was an an interview with Nelson Mandela. The journalist who conducted the interview described how it had been interrupted when somebody had walked through the door unannounced and that he and the 'Black Pimpernel' had hidden behind a curtain.

CHAPTER 4

Opening blasts of a liberation war

Until 16 December 1961 I suppose there was a period that might, in other circumstances, be described as a phoney war. But on that day everything for us changed as the first acts of sabotage announced by the newly formed armed wing of the Congress movement struck home. Umkhonto we Sizwe (MK), the 'Spear of the Nation', had arrived. One of the targets was the small power transformer on the corner of Red Square, very close to where I lived. There was a lot of activity and we all assembled to see the damage and to speculate in whispers about who might have been responsible. At the same time we were excited about this obvious turnaround from the passive campaign that had until then been mounted against the apartheid regime.

There were a lot of people around and I noticed one of the COD members, Gerard Ludi, standing with his girlfriend, whom I had met at parties and meetings. At the time there was a rumour going around in COD circles that the group had been infiltrated by the Special Branch and Ludi's behaviour made me uneasy: he was eyeing people around us and seemed to be trying to listen in on conversations that were going on around him; he looked creepy.

As I later discovered, my brother Joe and his COD comrade, Terry Bell, had the same feelings about Ludi, despite the fact that he was trusted to the extent that he had represented the COD abroad, had been entertained by anti-apartheid groups in Sweden and Holland, and had visited Moscow.

It wasn't that I or they thought there was anything suspicious about Ludi, we just didn't like or trust him. Joe and Terry also thought he was 'gutless', a bit of a coward. I remember remarking to Omar: 'I don't trust the guy.' Omar asked why and I replied that it was a gut feeling, but that he behaved strangely.

One of the COD members at the time who was suspected of being a member of the Special Branch was an Afrikaner named Oosthuizen, known to us only as 'Oosie'. I had met and worked with him on a number of occasions and really liked him. Oosie took the suspicion very personally. It seemed, in fact, to be based on nothing more than the fact that he came from an Afrikaans-speaking family. He was ostracised by his white comrades and eventually committed suicide, leaving a sad note of farewell. It was a tragic loss to the movement as there was no evidence of him being a spy.

Gerard Ludi on the other hand, was indeed an informer. Using what later transpired to have been a designation made up as a publicity stunt by his handlers, he gave evidence as 'secret agent QO18' against a number of Communist Party members who were also members of the COD.

My curiosity about who might have been responsible for the explosion was satisfied days later when I was working in the local library. Moosa Moosajee came into the building and furtively handed me a parcel. Taking me by the arm, he walked me towards the door and asked me to get rid of the parcel as soon as possible. He then retreated into the library and, as I reached the doorway, in walked two Special Branch officers.

As nonchalantly as I could, I strolled out and, as soon as I was out of sight, rushed home. In the privacy of my room, I opened the parcel. It contained soiled rubber gloves, wire cutters, packets of substances and plastic covers, and it smelled of flammable liquids. Shaken and frightened, I left the room and, with the parcel in my hand, jumped over the wall next to the flat where I had discovered a hole descending deep into the building. I dropped the parcel into the hole, knowing it would probably be impossible to retrieve it even if anyone knew it was there.

Later that evening I saw Moosajee and was relieved that he had not been arrested. We spoke in general terms, but the matter of the parcel was never discussed and I never asked what had happened after the Special Branch men entered the library. These were nerve-racking and sometimes frightening times, times when we all thought it wise not to talk or to ask questions about anti-government involvement.

By mid-1962 the leadership of the resistance movement had obviously decided that Omar, Magan and I were reliable and trustworthy. We were called to a meeting by Paul Joseph, one of the most highly respected local Congress leaders. He asked our opinions about armed struggle, especially in the light of the changes that were then evident. We listened eagerly as he asked us what contribution we thought we might like to make. It was clear to us, although there was no formal approach, that we were being invited to join Umkhonto we Sizwe. We were about to become members of a cell in the MK underground.

I think the three of us were immensely proud at that moment. We didn't give the slightest thought to the serious implications of being recruited and naively agreed that we were prepared to put our lives on the line. And so the meeting ended without any further information apart from the fact that another meeting would be arranged. We left, excited and more than slightly overwhelmed.

And so it was that at a subsequent meeting, and without any training or instruction in anything, let alone anything to do with the military or guerrilla warfare, we were asked to find targets to blow up. The specific point made was that we should not endanger human life. It was stressed that the object was to hit economic targets away from populated areas, a form of armed propaganda. Without any real experience other than our knowledge of the streets, we took earnestly to the task, travelling around late at night seeking possible targets that might have maximum economic or symbolic impact and not pose any danger to people.

After a number of excursions we identified three possible targets and met with Paul Joseph to report. The first was a power supply above the railway bridge separating Fordsburg from Vrededorp, an isolated spot. We reported that the best time would be well after midnight and before 4am, when no trains were running. We also reported that we had seen a number of people in the area who were looking very suspicious, and we had had to abandon our survey in haste. What we did not know at the time was that another cell was operating in the same area at the same time, carrying out the same sort of surveillance. This lack of shared information and co-ordination in the very early stages of the armed struggle revealed how amateurish the organisation was.

Our second suggested target was a number of electricity pylons in an open field of long grass dotted with bushes, and the third, in the city, was a huge government hay storage facility just behind Bree Street School and near the Braamfontein railway station. In those days some municipal carts were horse-drawn and the hay was intended for those horses and also, quite possibly, for police horses. The storage facility was not far from the local police station. Having given our report, we left, and it was several weeks before we were again summoned by Paul.

This time, Omar, Magan and I were told that we needed to revisit our third target and set a date to carry out the sabotage. We were taken by surprise, considering that we had only joined this supposedly armed rebellion a few months earlier. Besides, we had no training in sabotage. Nonetheless, I think all three of us were both excited and fearful about the job we were being asked to do. But it seemed straightforward enough; we would be provided with Molotov cocktails (petrol bombs) closer to the date of operation.

The three of us made many visits to the site, looking for all possible escape routes and noting potential problems, while ensuring that the facility was full of hay, so that our act would have maximum impact. At the same time, and although we never discussed it, I think Omar and Magan were as aware as I was that the consequences would be serious if we were caught. However, I think the overall feeling was one of pride that we had been given such responsibility.

The chosen date for the operation was 20 July 1962. Paul supplied us with two Molotov cocktails to be launched just after midnight. All we had to do, he said, was to light the cloth fuses in the necks of the bottles and throw them into the hay store. Not knowing much about the bombs, we handled the parcel containing the bottles with extreme care, fearing that if we dropped them they would blow up in our faces.

As we proceeded towards our target we passed the parcel between us several times, looking out for any police presence. It was a cold night and we did not utter a word. I was tense, my jaws tightly locked, my face muscles stretched to the limit. I glanced over to Magan and then to Omar: same body language. We crossed over Bree Street near Minty's fish and chip shop and entered the dark area along the side of the school. Omar passed the parcel to me and took up his position on the corner while Magan and I went across the darkened street opposite the target, put on our gloves – we knew about not leaving fingerprints – and took a bottle each, disposing of the wrapping.

Through the windows of the hay store we could make out a full consignment of hay stacked to the ceiling. Nearby was the police station, some of its windows well lit, others dark. It was quiet, and the silence was frightful. Omar was to signal to us by coughing and, as I waited, I prayed that the signal would not come. But then it did. There was a low cough. After some hesitation Magan and I lit the fuses and threw the cocktails at the windows. As I ran away I heard the sound of breaking glass.

Omar ran into a residential building, Magan into the school area, so he could slip out into a side road and into Bree Street. I made my way to the tunnel leading to Braamfontein station. We never looked back, but nothing seemed to have happened. In fact, nothing had happened. Our first and only venture into sabotage had been a failure. At our debriefing meeting with Paul there was no explanation and we never asked for one. He had collected the Molotov cocktails and handed them to us, so we assumed that it was a test exercise to see if we would go through with the operation.

This was the only potentially serious act of sabotage I was ever involved in – the other targets we had selected were passed on to another cell … with dire consequences. The cell was led by Reggie Vandeyar, with Shirish Nanubhai, Indres Naidoo and a man called Gamat Jardine, who had been recruited by Reggie. When the operation took place the police were waiting for the group. Indres was shot in the shoulder, Reggie and Shirish were caught, and Jardine, who turned out to be a police informer, disappeared. Indres, in severe pain, was taken to his home, where his mother and sisters were not allowed to touch him as he groaned in agony. The family stood by helplessly while the police searched the house for explosives before taking Indres off. He, Reggie and Shirish served ten-year sentences on Robben Island.

A few weeks after this incident our small cell was called to a meeting to discuss sending two volunteers for military training. We were not told where the training would take place other than that it would be outside South Africa. The external mission in what was then Tanganyika (now Tanzania) would make the final decision. On the basis of our family circumstances and the dependence of members of the family on each of us, Magan ruled himself out. So it was just Omar and me, and I was a bit concerned about Omar. Not only because he was the eldest son in the family, but also because he had, in the past, suffered from occasional bouts of illness that caused him to be bed bound. But he was determined to go. So we discussed what we would tell family and friends to allay suspicion if we suddenly left the country.

We soon realised that we could concoct a perfect excuse. At the end of 1961 a group of Asian teachers from Kenya, mainly from Mombasa, had visited what was then Tanganyika, Mozambique and South Africa. When they got to Johannesburg they contacted the Indian Congress to provide accommodation and meals for the duration of their stay. As executive members of the Youth Congress we were given the task of making all the arrangements for catering and accommodation. As a result, we became good friends of Gul, Bharti, Sudha and Ismail and had kept in touch with them over the months. I had heard from Gul that they were preparing for a trip to Egypt and had invited me to join them. This would add to our cover story, especially if we ended up being trained in Egypt. So we informed the people around us that we had been invited to visit Mombasa and would be leaving within the next few months.

The first hurdle was getting passports. Since we had been involved in various political activities and had attended anti-apartheid meetings there was a strong possibility that we had been listed by the police. But there was always the confusion of names, as I already knew from experience. The police also often misspelled names within the Indian community and mistook nicknames for the real thing. So we duly applied and hoped for the best because Paul said if we did not get passports we would have to leave the country illegally. If our passport applications were successful it would make our return from training easy and we could then blend back into the community without raising suspicion.

In the meantime, we started the ball rolling by writing to Gul suggesting a visit and asking about possible accommodation. We received a positive response. This correspondence confirmed our cover story. But then it struck us that we had better find out where we might be going, so we could take suitable clothing. Paul was unsure, but thought that we would probably be trained in countries such as Egypt or Cuba. This was a great relief to both of us, since we possessed no heavy winter wear and our families, both struggling to maintain themselves, could not be expected to give any help in this regard. So we settled down to wait to see what would happen with our passport applications. Surprisingly, and little more than a month after we had applied, our passports arrived. We were on our way.

As the date of our departure came closer Omar and I were concerned about the financial impact on our families. We thought we would ask a well-known figure in the movement to ensure that, if hard times befell our families, they would be helped by the movement. We were told bluntly that we were not part of a charitable organisation. This reply surprised us because it was known that when this person himself was in detention his family was well looked after by the 'not charitable movement'.

However, train tickets from Johannesburg to Durban and tickets for a sea passage from Durban to Mombasa were handed to us, and we were each given a £5 allowance and told that all other costs would be covered when we reached Dar es Salaam, where we were expected. The training would take six months and on our return to South Africa we would establish an underground unit.

On the afternoon of 7 October 1962 Omar and I were seen off at Johannesburg's Park railway station by my brother Joe and a large group of friends. We were bound for Durban to board the ship the SS *Karanja*, which would take us up the coast to Dar es Salaam and so to the movement's exile headquarters. As far as our friends were concerned, we would continue up the coast to Mombasa to spend time with the Asian teachers from Kenya who had visited us. And, of course, there was always the prospect of a side trip to Egypt. This would be covered by the small amount of money we had managed to save.

The same story was spun to the friends we stayed with in Durban and who came to the dockside to see us off. We had spread – often to the envy of friends and acquaintances – this tale of our invitation to visit Kenya. At the dockside we told my good friend Rabia and a relative, Baboo, along with Joe's girlfriend, Kamoo, that we would be away for 'a month or so'. Obviously our training would take a bit longer, but we could always cover that aspect by saying what a good time we were having in Kenya.

At least I was not completely in the dark about what to expect aboard the SS *Karanja*. It was the sister ship of the SS *Kampala* and both provided a regular, relatively inexpensive, service between South Africa and India. My brother Joe had travelled on the *Kampala* when he had left to study medicine in Mumbai, then still known as Bombay. Unfortunately, owing to a severe heart defect, he had had to curtail his studies. When he returned, he regaled us with stories of the ship and the trip.

The first shock we had when we went aboard was that we were told that only our fare had been paid. If we wanted to eat, we had to pay £5 each for our meals on the voyage, our entire allowance from the movement. We made our way down to the lower deck, where we were booked. It was a large area in the bowels of the ship with bunk beds and no cubicles, let alone cabins. The space held families of different sizes and a range of age groups.

There was a large common dining area with no tables or chairs, only mats on the floor, where we sat and ate our meals. The division was based on religious requirements and the waiter would announce: 'People of Muslim faith your meal is ready,' and so on. Since the lower deck was so close to the engine room it was also very hot. Omar and I and a few of the younger passengers sought relief by making our way to the upper deck to catch the breeze. In the process we made friends with a number of girls from Cape Town who were on their way to India and who were booked in on the upper deck. When the ship's officers locked the doors to the upper deck to prevent us from coming up for air, the girls would let us in.

All of this was far from idyllic, especially for me. Almost from the time we left Durban harbour I was seasick. Apart from occasionally slipping up to the top deck for fresh air, I spent most of the time at sea lying on my bunk, unable to eat. I found relief only when we reached port, any port.

And there were a number of stops as we made our way up the east coast of Africa: Lourenço Marques (now Maputo), known generally as LM; Beira; and Port Mozambique, before we reached Dar es Salaam. The *Karaja* then went on to Zanzibar and, finally, Mombasa. As soon as the ship docked I would rush ashore to spend most of the time walking around and eating.

Fortunately, near most of the docks, there was a fish and chip shop. So, no problem about being halaal, although most of these meals were not like those at Akhalwaya's in Fordsburg: the chilli was missing. I was also careful how much I ate because, once back on the ship, I would lie in misery, looking forward to the next port.

The first stop was LM, a very popular holiday port for white South Africans. Since Mozambique was a Portuguese colony there was far greater mixing of people of colour than in South Africa, although not necessarily full equality economically and socially. I spent my hurried and brief time ashore and noticed as we sailed out of the harbour that more passengers had embarked.

One of them was a young lad who claimed he was from the militant north Indian Pathan clan. He boasted how strong he was and brandished a knife as he intimidated the passengers on the lower deck. Their complaints to members of the crew were ignored and Omar and I initially kept our distance. However, at one point we nearly got into a fight with him, but one of the girls from Cape Town intervened and stopped us. We also decided that, since we were on a mission, we should not jeopardise it. We would try to avoid the belligerent Pathan.

I was, in any event, hardly fit for any fight once the ship put out to sea. The pitching and rolling had me huddled on my bunk or staring forlornly over the rail on the upper deck. Beira, I recall, was only a 12-hour stop, barely enough time for me to recover. And Port Mozambique was an even shorter stop. That was the fourth day of our voyage and I was getting desperate, looking forward to being able to disembark in Dar es Salaam and leave sea travel for good.

After what sometimes seemed like an eternity, we finally tied up alongside the dock in Dar es Salaam on the night of 14 October. The pitching and rolling stopped and I was able to sleep. For the first time since boarding the SS *Karanja* I managed to have a decent breakfast that morning. But then came further delays because of some immigration difficulties before we were finally allowed to disembark. We had arrived. Omar and I were about to set out on our final journey to become fully fledged fighters for the liberation of our country.

We were light-hearted when we stepped ashore. There was no-one to meet us, but we did not really expect anyone and we had been given the address of the ANC office. On the dockside we asked for directions and were told that the centre of town was not far off; we could walk.

As we strode out of the docklands I think we both imagined the warm welcome we would receive. We would enter the office and ask, as we had been told to, for 'Comrade Oliver Tambo', the acting president of the ANC, and announce that we were reporting for military training.

We found the office easily enough, but when we entered, the four people inside regarded us with looks bordering on hostility. Where were we from? Who had sent us? What were we doing there? There was no mention of Oliver Tambo. It was clear that nobody knew anything about us. The four men in the office, and others who came in from time to time, kept asking the same questions over and over. Every so often one of them would disappear into what appeared to be a back office, only to reappear to start quizzing us again. All of this was accompanied by a lot of whispering. It was total confusion.

We were hungry, but no food was offered, although we were each given a Coke to drink. It was getting on into the afternoon when a woman walked into the office from the street. I recognised her immediately: it was Pam Beira, someone I had worked with on a number of campaigns in South Africa. She also recognised me – and seemed even more surprised than I was at meeting up in Dar. She and a black journalist, Joe Louw, had been arrested for contravening the Immorality Act. Rather than go to trial and face possibly lengthy prison sentences, they had fled the country separately and made their way to Dar es Salaam. Pam sat down beside me and I explained why we were there and how we had got there, while also updating her on events in South Africa since she had left.

When I had explained what had happened, Pam went into the back office and we heard the murmurs of a long discussion with a number of people, although we couldn't hear what was being said. But the upshot was that we were finally introduced to Jimmy Hadebe, one of the comrades who had questioned us. We discovered that he was the head of the ANC mission. Jimmy explained that the South African Special Branch was sending people out to infiltrate the organisation and the ANC had to be very security conscious when people like us turned up unannounced.

They had apparently received no information about us, but were satisfied with the assurances from Pam. Unfortunately, Tambo was abroad and the Dar es Salaam office could not take any decisions without 'consulting OR'. Under these circumstances it would be advisable for us to continue our journey to Mombasa and the movement would be in touch and would instruct us when to return. And so we were taken by car to the harbour, where we bade farewell to Pam and Jimmy and made our way back to the SS *Karanja*, feeling, to put it mildly, rather disappointed.

The ship was leaving for Zanzibar the next morning and that evening Omar and I were sitting on deck when three men appeared at the dockside and started boarding the ship. We recognised Jimmy Hadebe, but not the other two, and went across to the gangplank to meet them. We were really excited, thinking they had come to collect us. Obviously, we thought, they must have received news from South Africa after we had left the office.

We barely concealed our excitement when Hadebe introduced us to Tennyson and Ambrose Makiwane. He suggested we take them to the bar where we could chat and, as we went up the deck stairway, we bumped into Mr Pathan. He seemed shocked to see us with the three comrades, turned around and rushed off in the opposite direction.

At the bar the three ordered whisky and it was obvious that we were expected to pay. We obliged, although we were concerned since this was not part of our budget and when we left Durban, we had only had about £40 between us. However, as we saw it, this was likely to be the end of the journey, so we paid when more drinks were ordered and waited for the news we wanted to hear. It never came. After some general chat, the three stood up, wished us well ... and left. We were depressed, but came to realise later that one good thing had come about because of that meeting: Mr Pathan stayed well out of our way throughout the rest of the voyage.

CHAPTER 5

And so to Mombasa

We were not in the best of spirits as the ship sailed out of Dar, heading for Zanzibar. For me, however, the trip was mercifully brief and the sea not too choppy. As I stood on the deck, the smell of cloves wafted across the ocean long before we anchored, there being no port. Instead, we were ferried to the island in small boats for a welcome four-hour stopover. Short as it was, we managed to explore the alleyways of Stone Town, admiring the Arab architecture, sampling the food and even experiencing the smooth white sand of the beaches. Then it was back on board to face more pitching and rolling on the way to Mombasa.

We reached the Kenyan port on the afternoon of 16 October ... and were not allowed to disembark. The immigration officers, who were all British, questioned us at length about what we were doing, where we had come from and what we intended to do. Finally, they allowed us to use the telephone and we had Gul's number. When he heard of our predicament he rushed over and, after a conversation with the immigration officials, signed a form accepting full responsibility for our stay. Led by Gul, we picked up our belongings and left the ship.

Gul worked as an accountant at an Islamic Education Institute that provided him with a two-bedroom flat. Omar and I would share his spare bedroom. He also had a servant who did all the cooking, did our washing and ironing, and otherwise took good care of us.

Sitting around in the flat on that first evening, Omar and I – we had worked out a suitable 'cover' story – explained that we were on a mission to get some information for the Dar offices of the ANC; that the trip to Mombasa was a cover, and that we would be returning to Dar in two weeks. As far as the people back home were concerned, we were on holiday. I also penned a letter to the Dar office giving our address in Mombasa and a telephone number where we could be contacted. It was promptly posted.

Gul was aware that we belonged to the Congress movement and he assumed we had been assigned to a low-level political visit. He would go along with the holiday story and he insisted on taking us to meet the teachers who had visited us in South Africa. Invitations flowed in thick and fast and we arranged to spend time with each of them. Over the next two weeks we were royally entertained as I waited for a response to the letter I had sent to the Dar office.

But two weeks passed and there was no response from the ANC. I sent another letter, asking for an urgent response, while Omar and I tried to keep a low profile, not wishing to abuse the hospitality we had been accorded. After all, we were supposed to be on our way home. So, for another two weeks we spent a lot of time walking around Mombasa or strolling along the beachfront, which seemed to be very popular among the locals, with families and young children running around, having fresh coconut drinks and eating hot, spicy nuts. With our very limited financial resources there was little we could do to entertain ourselves, but we were not about to divulge this information to our hosts and cause any embarrassment to ourselves.

As we moved into the fourth week of our stay, and still with no response from the ANC, Omar and I decided that we had to return to Dar es Salaam. We explained to Gul that we had to go to Dar and would like to leave most of our clothing with him as we would travel light. He agreed to keep our belongings and to forward them to us when we contacted him. The trouble then was how to get to Dar. Gul suggested that we go by bus, with a stopover in Tanga, a small port on the coast of Tanganyika, where we would have to stay overnight. Fortunately, he had a friend, Salim, who ran a business in Tanga and who would be able to accommodate us.

That journey from Mombasa to Tanga, a distance of about 208km, took four hours, since the road was not tarred and some parts of it qualified only as a track. But, as Gul had assured us, there were no problems with immigration. In fact, there were no immigration controls on this route. However, we had to dig into our depleted finances to pay for the bus tickets.

So it was that we set off from Mombasa at midday in the November heat. The bus was two-thirds full and Omar and I occupied seats at the rear. Gul's servant had prepared two parcels of bread, butter and jam sandwiches and included some Coke bottles filled with water for the journey. My seasickness experience had taught me to be prepared. I made sure that I had a large number of strong brown paper bags in case of an emergency. It was just as well, because there was no air conditioning in the bus and it was the height of summer. The heat was intense, but I still felt quite settled as the first kilometres ticked by.

However, after about 90 minutes, the nausea again made itself felt. The heat and the rocking motion of the bus as it rumbled over unmade roads was just too much for me. I tried my best to overcome the feeling and didn't want to resort to using my paper bags, but eventually I got up and staggered to the front of the bus. I asked the driver to stop, motioning that I was going to throw up. He spoke to me in Swahili. I responded in English. He laughed, but he did stop and I got off just in time. Five minutes later, with me feeling slightly better, the journey continued.

There were another four stops at small towns and villages before we reached Tanga and, at each of these, I would be the first passenger to alight and would walk around until the driver announced that he was again ready to leave. With an empty stomach I was not likely to embarrass myself. Besides, I did have my brown paper bags. But I had to endure a smiling Omar, who happily munched away at the food that had been packed for us.

We reached Tanga at around 5pm. It was a small town and Gul had said that our contact lived near the cinema and that it was a place where all the Asian families knew each other. All we would have to do to track down Salim and his family would be to approach any person of Asian origin and ask for the home of Salim Bowla. How right he was. The first person of Asian appearance we saw, we asked – and were taken straight to the Bowla home and business. We entered and introduced ourselves and Salim welcomed us, saying he was expecting us – Gul had sent on word ahead.

We met the Bowla family, a lovely wife and two children, a son and a teenage daughter, who all made us feel very much at home. They fed us and then took us around the town and to the beachfront. The whole area was beautiful and the people friendly. We were beset by questions about South Africa and the political situation and had to play it very low-key. Salim wondered why we were going to Dar. We said we were returning to South Africa and hoped to take the ship back from Dar.

After a good night's sleep I woke refreshed, but in dread of the journey to Dar, which would also, we had been told, take about four hours over very rough roads. Washed and fed on biryani, chicken curry and homemade roti, we were presented with a similar spread of food and drink for the next leg of our journey. It was 10am when we took leave of our hosts, exchanging invitations to visit South Africa and revisit Tanga. The only concern we had was that we would arrive in Dar after the ANC office had closed for the day. Then we would have no place to stay and would have no idea where to go.

As usual, as we trundled out of Tanga, I was unable to enjoy the food. I had deliberately had very little to eat for breakfast and had explained why to Salim. He laughed and assured me that I would be okay. I was not. At the first stop in a nearby village I threw up and dreaded getting back onto the bus. Like the previous vehicle, it was very hot, with no air conditioning, and it was packed. I was, however, able to nod off from time to time between bouts of nausea, and it was good to have Omar beside me: we had formed an even closer friendship and were both buoyed up by the thought that we would be heading home after some real training.

So it was that we arrived in Dar at about 3pm and made our way to the ANC office. Our reception was not exactly welcoming. Quite the opposite: the comrades in the office seemed shocked to see us. Jimmy Hadebe was there and we were not introduced to the others – 'for security reasons', we were later told.

While we waited the group got into a huddle in the back office while we sat in bemused silence in the outer office. But we were at least given some soft drinks. Eventually Jimmy emerged and took us to his house, where we met his wife and some young children. There we were offered some food – meat and rice, which we refused politely because we were not sure if the meat was halaal.

In any event, we still had the remains of the parcel of food we had been given in Tanga and we knew that it should be eaten before it went bad. Jimmy left and said he would call later. The conversation around us was in one of the vernacular African languages which neither Omar nor I understood. We also had a sense that we were being discussed and this made us very uncomfortable, so we tried to make light of this by suggesting that we should start conversing in Gujarati to get even. But this would not have worked: my knowledge of Gujarati was very limited. It was Omar's mother tongue, while my mother spoke Urdu.

We didn't feel particularly welcome and spent most of the afternoon sitting on the front steps of the house trying to figure out what was happening. We had been given no information and when we had asked about Oliver Tambo we were told that he was still out of the country. Neither of us thought that the movement we had joined could be incompetent. I remember telling Omar that it must be because we had landed unexpectedly; there must be a transit point where people arriving for training were put up and that was where we should have gone. After all, that was what Paul Joseph had implied before we left.

At around 5pm Jimmy came back home and told us to get into his car. We jumped to it, convinced that we would now be taken to the transit point. After about half an hour we pulled up in front of a house. I suppose it was a transit point of sorts, because the door opened and Pam Beira came out and hugged me. At the same time, Jimmy said that we would be staying with Pam while arrangements were being made for us to be sent for training. At least things were moving.

That evening Omar went to bed early and I sat outside with Pam and explained what had happened to us. She confessed that she had not been given any information about us and that she was also treated with suspicion, because everyone seemed aware that the South African Special Branch had been sending out people to infiltrate the movement. Strict security measures obviously had to be taken, but there seemed to be a problem with communication: the ANC had not received confirmation about Omar and me and until this was verified we would be staying with Pam.

Over the next two weeks Omar and I spent a great deal of time walking around Dar. We wanted to become familiar with our surroundings, but we also did not have the money for any other transport. We speculated constantly about what might have happened. What could have gone wrong? Had Paul Joseph not sent on the information about us? We had no contact with the ANC office because Pam had advised us to stay away; we should wait for Jimmy to make the next move. However, we still sent our postcards home to maintain the illusion that we were tourists at large.

But, especially in the mornings and early evenings, we learned some valuable lessons. We became domesticated, helping with the cleaning, assisting in the preparation of meals, and doing our washing and ironing. This was a big change from our home setup and from the time spent in Mombasa, where everything was done for us.

It made us especially aware of how we had taken our sisters for granted; they had always waited on us and we had never lifted a spoon to help out. This was the culture in the community and when we became involved politically these issues were not raised. All the men, including those who recruited us and were responsible for our political development, lived in exactly the same way: male dominance was accepted as the norm.

As political activists in Fordsburg, we had been given lessons in Marxism by Ahmed Kathrada, better known as 'Kathy'. Even in his lectures the issue of gender roles was not taken up. But we thought we might have done him a disservice because he had gone underground and the classes were suspended. Perhaps, had they not been interrupted, we would have covered this topic and even questioned the way we were living.

I also discovered some other aspects about myself in that brief period in Dar. One incident that stands out was when Omar and I were walking around one day and bumped into one of the locals of African origin. He asked me what language I spoke at home and I proudly informed him that my mother tongue was Urdu. He had studied in Pakistan and he promptly switched to Urdu. I was totally lost. I made some sense of what he was saying, but quickly realised that my vocabulary was sorely lacking. I froze and could not respond. My knowledge of Urdu was clearly very limited, since I only ever spoke the language with my mother, because she was uncomfortable with English. But these were conversations limited to greetings, acknowledgements and asking for food and pocket money. I would also often lapse into English, although she would always reply in Urdu. Omar, on the other hand, seemed to speak Gujarati quite fluently.

Walking, sitting around, even doing household chores gave me a lot of time to think. And these issues of gender roles and of household status and language occupied a lot of my time. But then, suddenly, it seemed the waiting was over: Jimmy arrived at the house one morning and told us to bring our passports and accompany him to the office. There was no hesitation on our part. We ran inside, grabbed our passports and jumped into the waiting car that took us to the ANC office.

As we entered the office we saw more people than usual, but there were no introductions as we handed over our passports and were led to the inner office. There, at last, was Oliver Tambo. We were formally introduced and he shook our hands and asked us to be seated in front of him. He sat silently for some time, apparently sizing us up, his eyes moving first to Omar then to me. His expression was stern and I felt a little uncomfortable because he did not appear to be friendly.

OR questioned us for about an hour. He wanted to know exactly where we came from and we had to tell him in detail about how we were recruited and how we came to be in Dar. There was no indication of whether we were believed or not and OR informed us that there was still no confirmation from South Africa. However, he assured us that the ANC hoped to get some news soon and we should return to Pam's house. The movement would be in touch. And so we returned to the house with some relief, because Pam, although she also had very little information, at least made me feel at ease.

It was mid-week and Pam raised our spirits somewhat when she announced that she was giving a party on the Saturday night. There would be lots of interesting people coming, she said. We would be able to meet members of other liberation movements such as the Zimbabwe African People's Union (ZAPU), the Mozambique Liberation Front (Frelimo) and the Popular

Movement for the Liberation of Angola (MPLA). Also in Dar at the time were a number of African Americans who came to the continent to meet African leaders and people from the liberation movements.

In South Africa we had been starved of information about these groups and individuals, deprived by means of state censorship. I suppose we were rather overawed at the party and were, in any event, merely part of the crowd. We also had no idea of the significance of any individuals, and even when Pam mentioned to me the following day that Malcolm X had been present, at one stage standing alongside Omar and me, it didn't mean anything. It was only years later that I realised the opportunity I had missed to shake hands with one of the icons of struggle.

We were, perhaps understandably, also preoccupied with our own concerns. We had been away from home for more than six weeks and were still walking around Dar, waiting. Paul had assured us that we would be away for no more than six months. Time was slipping away. However, we kept sending postcards to the family telling them of our supposed travels, but not providing any forwarding addresses. Maybe, we sometimes thought, we would be sent back to South Africa without any training.

Then one afternoon Jimmy came over to Pam's house and again took us to the office. It seemed obvious that, at last, something positive was in store. It was, but it was the last thing we expected. After being told to wait in the outer office while Jimmy consulted with others in the back, we were told: 'Pack your bags and be ready to leave tomorrow for London.'

With that, Jimmy handed us back our passports, along with tickets for a bus trip to Nairobi and another to Juba in the Sudan. He explained that there was an overnight stay in Nairobi and then we would go on to Juba, from where we would fly to Benghazi in Libya and on to Luxembourg. We would then travel by train to Ostend, take a ferry to Harwich and then take another train to London. We were also given a telephone number that we were to call when we reached the British capital. We should speak to Vella Pillay, who would meet us and would explain what would happen next.

With a wodge of tickets and our passports in our hands and having taken note of the instructions, we were told to be ready at 9.30am the next morning when we would be picked up and taken to the bus station to start our journey. But how were we to survive? No trouble, we were told, everything is paid for. Bewildered, Omar and I were dropped back at Pam's house. No-one was home yet and we sat on the steps for some time trying desperately to work out what was happening. Surely we could not expect military training in Britain?

I worried aloud about this. If Dar was the transit point for all the people coming out to be sent for military training, why were we being sent to London of all places? As usual, Omar smiled and said nothing. In our relationship, which had developed over the years, I would take the lead on anything current while Omar was always willing to discuss issues of home and the past. Unlike me, he was also consistent in his religious practice and would perform his prayers daily and read the Quran. I, on the other hand, would skip the practice from time to time. Omar was also much more accepting and content with what life seemed to throw at us.

When Pam came home, I related what had happened. Like Omar and me, she was taken aback and could not make any sense of why we were being sent to London. She also confirmed that all the people who had so far come through Dar had been sent for training to North Africa. This, to me, meant Egypt. There were other ANC people staying at the house and I could hear Pam having sometimes heated discussions. I assumed they were about us and the way we had been treated.

As Omar and I packed, we were mainly conscious that December would mean winter in the UK. What clothes we had were light and suitable for summer wear in the heat and humidity of places like Dar. We each had a sleepless night and I went over and over in my mind how I would cope with this newly proposed long journey, especially given my record of motion sickness. There was also the possibility of problems with immigration, because we had not been provided with visas for any of the countries we were supposed to pass through. What would happen if we were denied entry?

I tried to understand the ANC's reasoning and wondered whether they had considered the likely barriers we might confront. What would happen if, because of a lack of money, we were turned back at any borders? How would we get back? In the end, the best I could do for myself was to stuff my hand luggage with brown bags in the event that I needed to throw up. That, at least, was something that was bound to happen.

That morning, before Pam left for work, she came in to say goodbye and gave me some addresses of friends in London to contact if we needed them. She also gave me 50 shillings as pocket money and hugged me and Omar. We thanked her for the hospitality and her support and the comfort she had given us whenever we were feeling down. That was the last time I saw Pam, but I kept in touch about her through a number of channels. I know that Joe Louw also came to Dar, but later left for the United States, while Pam stayed on. She eventually married Marcelino dos Santos, who was the deputy president of Frelimo and, after independence, held various Cabinet posts in the government of Mozambique.

Omar had packed some cheese and egg sandwiches for the trip, along with a couple of bottles of Coke and water. He and I waited on the steps until we were picked up by Jimmy and taken to the bus station in the centre of Dar. There we were dropped off with a casual handshake. Initially unsure what to do, we stood with our bags and watched Jimmy drive off before eventually making our way to an office to enquire about our bus to Nairobi. We were directed to an area from where, we were told, the bus would leave and, in due course, a bus arrived. The driver assured us he was heading for Nairobi. We were finally on our way. Only we were not too sure where to.

CHAPTER 6

Journey to the UK

We boarded the bus in Dar, took the rear seats and settled in, the only non-African passengers travelling. But we struck up a conversation with a friendly Tanzanian who spoke fluent English. He was heading for Nairobi, a trip he had made many times, and asked where we were headed. 'London,' we said, as if it was right next door and the most logical place to be going.

The remaining seats in the bus were quickly filled by people of all ages, often carrying piles of luggage and live chickens in baskets. Even before the bus left, the atmosphere was stuffy and when our newfound friend said that we would only arrive in Nairobi at about midday the following day, I felt decidedly queasy. But he assured us the journey of about 800km provided some magnificent views, especially if the weather remained dry. We would stop at Arusha and Moshi, in an area dominated by the snow-capped peak of Mt Kilimanjaro. I remained apprehensive.

I was sure I was not going to need much of the food Omar had packed. And so it proved. For me, the journey was another awful experience. But Omar and our Tanzanian friend shared the food and chatted away. Omar at least had better company than just me for a change. I did manage to doze off from time to time and, whenever the bus stopped to drop off or pick up passengers, I would go for a walk, always asking the driver to ensure that I was not left behind. And it was always the same driver. I never thought anything of it at the time, but years later I wondered how those drivers managed to cover vast distances on their own on what were often little more than tracks.

With hindsight, I also regret not having known then more about the countries we travelled through, the people, culture, language, geography, politics and history. I never even appreciated the beauty of the wild countryside, the splendour of Mt Kilimanjaro, and the sight of Nandi Hills, all fascinating landmarks that I now acknowledge. But, in my defence, our education system and our focus on the anti-apartheid struggle had not prepared us to appreciate much of the wider world. And then, of course, there was my physical and, at times, mental state throughout that journey.

So I endured my usual discomfort, oblivious to much that was going on around me, and we reached Nairobi at about midday without incident. The bus station was close to a market area and our Tanzanian friend sought directions to our hotel. It turned out to be a 20-minute walk, so we said our goodbyes and Omar and I set off across Nairobi. We found the hotel without much trouble, but we still had no idea what arrangements had been made, where we would stay in the days ahead, and what we would eat and drink. Jimmy had simply picked us up and dropped us off with vouchers and airline tickets. All we knew was that London was our final destination.

At the hotel we were directed to an office where we were asked for our airline tickets. There, as the officials processed our documents, we discovered that we were on a package tour, inclusive of accommodation, bus and air fares. Meals, apart from breakfast, were not included. We could at least look forward to breakfast the next morning and, with the money Pam had given us, we could buy other food. The hotel was also comfortable. We showered, changed into clean clothes, and ventured out into the Kenyan capital.

I had not eaten for 36 hours and was very hungry. Making sure we could retrace our steps, Omar and I walked toward the market area where the bus had dropped us. We had noticed restaurants on the way to the hotel and we soon discovered that most were halaal. We chose one that was almost entirely vegetarian and I recall that it cost just two and a half shillings for a most enjoyable meal of dhal (lentils) and rice as well as aloo gobi (spiced potato and cauliflower) and another spicy potato dish. The meal was only slightly spoiled for me by the fact that I was aware that it would probably be my last for some time.

Back at the hotel that evening we met up with other members of the package tour party. The 35 travellers came from all over East Africa – from Uganda, Tanzania and Kenya. They were mainly Asians, among them Goans, and a group of white people. There was not a single African in the party and each group kept to itself in what we recognised as the apartheid pattern. Omar and I got to talking to some of the people from Mombasa, telling them how we had enjoyed ourselves in the seaside town. There was no language barrier and I felt comfortable with people who seemed to share a similar background. For a change, I was almost looking forward to the journey, but took the precaution of not following Omar, who had a hearty breakfast.

As we stood about on the pavement outside the hotel waiting for our bus, it suddenly dawned on me that we were going to travel through Kenya and Uganda and into Sudan. That journey would take anywhere between 24 and 30 hours, and by mid-morning, it was already very warm. I had to persuade myself that this trip would be less problematic for me than the others. But I started feeling very unsure.

I had overheard one of the tourists the previous day saying that the worst place to be seated on a bus was at the back. This was over the rear wheels and when the bus hit pot holes the impact was felt more in the rear seats. For a more comfortable ride the seats in the middle were best. So Omar and I decided to ensure we got middle seats. When the bus arrived, my spirits were lifted a bit more: this was not one of the rather battered old busses we had travelled in before, it was a modern coach.

We quickly got aboard, securing seats in the middle. They were soft and contoured. This, I was sure, would all make for a much more pleasant journey, even if there was no air conditioning. However, I was also aware that many of the roads we would travel on would be rutted and rough and that when it rained they could become extremely treacherous. So far, in our journeyings on the continent, there had been no rain. Long may that continue, I hoped.

In any event, we had more to concern us than potholes, treacherous roads and my queasy stomach. There were bound to be border crossings and we knew, especially from our experience when we arrived in Mombasa, that immigration authorities request visas and guarantees before allowing entry. We had nothing stamped in our passports and the thought of being stranded at some border post in the middle of East Africa was more than a little worrying.

But whether it was the seats in the middle or the well-made, tarred roads leading out of Nairobi, I was feeling much better as the coach headed east. We had been told that the distance to Kampala at that time was estimated to be around 885km and the travelling time was 18 hours, depending on road conditions. If there was any rain before or during the journey this would increase the travelling time and some roads might become impassable, which would create problems for us in getting to Juba in time for our flight.

By late afternoon, as we were leaving the last town in Kenya and the roads had become rougher, I could feel nausea coming on, probably further contributed to by the thought of arriving at the border and meeting up with immigration authorities. Omar and I kept our conversations about this to a minimum in case we were overheard and raised any suspicions. We whispered softly between ourselves, speculating on what might happen and what stories we would tell.

But as the day drew to a close we suddenly realised, given the hours we had been travelling, that we must have been in Uganda for some time. Yet there had been no sign of any border and the various stops made along the way meant nothing to us since the only Ugandan town we knew of was Kampala, the capital. With the realisation that, somehow, we had made it into Uganda I could feel the pressure lifting and my nausea easing.

We made very good time, but it was late when we reached Kampala, where there would be a two hour stop. The town was almost deserted apart from the passengers waiting for the Juba connection and a few policemen hanging around. Omar and I tried to stay out of sight of the police just in case they decided to ask us for documents. But nobody paid us any attention and when the coach arrived we quickly boarded.

It had been a stressful day and I must have been very tired because I remember dozing off. Omar, too, fell asleep, because when I woke up his head was on my shoulder. It was still dark, I had no idea where we were and most of the other passengers were asleep. I checked the time: just after 4am. Then, as I settled down to try to catch up on some more sleep, I realised that we would soon be coming to another border and Sudan did not enjoy the same close relationship with other countries as did Uganda, Kenya and Tanzania. Omar carried on sleeping peacefully and I realised that, ridiculous as it seemed, I was the one worrying for both of us.

While these thoughts were going through my mind, the bus stopped. It was early morning, with the dark outside turning to light grey, and I could hear voices in languages I did not understand. The group leader from the Nairobi travel agency moved up the bus, waking passengers and asking for passports. Nervously, I woke Omar and we handed over the documents. The group leader collected Tanzanian, Ugandan, Kenyan and British passports from the other passengers. Ours were the only South African documents and I thought this might be a problem, but the group leader seemed unconcerned.

As he left the bus, carrying the pile of passports, I realised that I was in no shape, mentally or physically, to make up any stories about what we were doing there and how we came to be heading for London. For the first time I also saw a worried look on Omar's face. We had no idea where we were or which country's immigration officials would be looking at our documents. Time ticked by extremely slowly as I tried to hear what the other passengers on the coach were saying, hoping that they might at least know on which side of the border we were and what might be happening.

At previous stops I had invariably been the first one off, but here I stayed put. Which was probably just as well, because I noticed that none of the other passengers had left their seats. Only the tour leader, with all our documents, had left. Then he suddenly appeared and walked down the length of the coach, handing back the passports. I know that my hands were shaking as I took back the documents. The tour leader then walked to his seat at the front of the coach, the engine started up, and we were on our way again. The relief I felt then was an experience I'll always remember. I even felt hungry and wanted to eat and drink, it was like a celebration, until I realised that I was still not sure which border post we had passed. I turned to another passenger and asked him. 'Sudan,' he said, and the relief surged back. It took perhaps another eight hours before we finally reached Juba, but it was, for me, the most relaxed I had been on any of our road and sea trips.

Juba was a small town that reminded me of something out of a Western. But it did have a hotel with the basic facilities. We were given food and once again Omar and I were concerned about the meat being halaal, but we were assured by other Muslims in the party that it was. Although the accommodation was basic, with the two of us sharing a room, the hotel provided mosquito nets over the beds, something we had not enjoyed in either Tanzania or Kenya, where the means of keeping these insects at bay was to burn a pyrethrum coil. We had eventually got used to the smell – and it was better than being bitten.

There not being much to see in Juba, we did not venture out. In any event, we were very tired and went to sleep early. Our flight was scheduled to leave at midday and we wanted to be fresh, especially since neither of us had flown before and we were quite nervous. My first thought was about being airsick – having been seasick and land sick it would complete the circle. However, I felt that I was getting used to travelling and to my reaction to motion. The last leg of the journey had been a great improvement.

We woke early in the morning to hear the buzzing of mosquitos around the nets, which gradually subsided as the sun came up. Omar was first up and said his prayers. I felt guilty and showered and did the same. Since being on the road we had not had time or a place to pray, but Omar always took the opportunity and I would join him. I reflected that it was a blessing that Omar was around because I would not always be conscious of this need.

At breakfast, and just in case, not knowing what air travel would bring, I remember I had two slices of dry toast and a cup of tea. The tour leader then assembled us and took our passports, and we boarded the coach for the airport. It was just a single stretch of tarmac on which was parked a four-engine propeller plane. To the side were a few buildings. To us, this Air Luxembourg aircraft seemed big, and we were staring at it when another coach pulled up with more passengers, mainly of European origin. There must have been nearly 100 of us who filed up the steps and were directed to seats, where we were again handed our passports and the remaining travel documents.

As soon as I sat down, I noticed in the pocket in the seat in front of me were small bags. I knew what these were for from the stories I heard from people who had flown before. I showed them to Omar, who laughed and said that they were obviously expecting me. As we taxied to the end of the airstrip at midday, we were informed that the flight time to Benghazi was six hours. For the first couple of those hours I felt well. But then we struck what I later learnt was called turbulence and the nausea returned; the bags were handy. I had now been sick on all forms of transport and I resolved that I had to get over this problem. The turbulence, my stomach and my state of mind settled and I dozed off until we landed in Benghazi.

As we stepped out of the plane a cold breeze hit us. We were still dressed in our summer attire and the light raincoats we had brought from South Africa. We were freezing and dashed for the building we were directed to. It was dark as we entered the building and were shown to the transit area, which housed a restaurant displaying a large portrait of King Idris, the first and only king of Libya after independence in 1951. I was in no mood to eat, so we sat out the four-hour stopover until we were summoned again to the plane. This meant another dash across the tarmac. It was past midnight, a biting cold wind was still blowing and, to cap it all, there was a sudden downpour of rain. We rushed to the plane, soaked and shivering.

At least the plane was warm and my stomach had settled, so I slept most of the way. However, my nerves started playing up again as we came in to land: here certainly there must be immigration and not only did we have South African passports, we also had just £46 between us. Omar seemed quite unconcerned as we made our way to the immigration area at Luxembourg airport, where we presented our passports. But they were stamped without comment and we were waved through to collect our bags and meet up again with the rest of the touring party.

The tour leader told us that we would leave immediately for the station, to take a train to Ostend in Belgium, followed by a ferry crossing to Harwich and then a train to London. I had a chat with him and discovered that he was going to accompany us to London. This was a relief, especially since we still had two borders to cross: into Belgium and Britain. So far we had been really lucky, but I recalled the grilling we had been given when we reached Mombasa, and it was British immigration officers who had caused the problem.

Before leaving the airport for the train station, Omar and I put on extra layers of vests and shirts and wore our raincoats. These kept us reasonably warm until we got onto the train bound for Ostend. By then we had met and started talking to some fellow travellers from Mombasa. We chatted in general terms, always on guard not to appear anything but holidaymakers or, in my case, to reveal my fears about facing the immigration authorities.

As the train moved out of the station I caught sight of what I was told were television aerials protruding across the skyline. So many, and on just about every home. I was fascinated because, at the time, South Africa did not have television, the government being concerned that such a medium might have the wrong impact, especially on the black population.

It was a great journey. For the first time since leaving Dar I felt warm and comfortable travelling. I lost track of time just staring out of the window as the scenery flashed by, and we passed through small towns and villages. I had never anticipated travelling in Europe and this was all a new experience. The only lingering fear was Belgian immigration. But there was none and the train pulled in to Brussels, where we had to change trains for Ostend. The tour leader went off and came back with some refreshments as we waited. The train pulled in, we all got on and I must have dozed off immediately, because the next thing I knew we were entering the port area of Ostend.

The ferry, we noticed, was not as big as the SS *Karanja*, and we were surprised to see trucks and cars driving on to it. Their headlights were on because it was already getting dark, but, when I looked at my watch, it was just after 3pm. And it was cold.

Perhaps the North Sea is sometimes calm. That day it wasn't. Thirty minutes out of the harbour, with the ferry rolling and pitching, I was clinging to the railings with the cold, wet wind slashing against me, trying all the time to think clearly and not fall overboard. It was the worst part of our four-day journey. Fearful of losing my grip on the railings, I charged down to find a toilet on the lower deck. Along a passage my way was blocked by a staggering man. He reeled into me and I threw up on him. But he was so drunk that he did not realise what I had done. Eventually the pitching and rolling stopped as we reached Harwich. It was 24 November and both Omar and I were exhausted.

As we waited to disembark even Omar looked a bit fearful when we stood in a line with all the other passengers waiting to approach the immigration desk. Finally, it was our turn. The officer took our passports, gave us a smile, flipped through the documents and stamped them. We smiled back and walked out of the area – and into England.

Finally, we were on our way to London. The train journey was uneventful, but when we reached Victoria station all the currency exchange facilities were closed and we had no local money. Fortunately, one of our fellow passengers happened to pass at that point and I told him about our problem. He fished out a three-penny coin. It was all I would need for a local call, he said.

CHAPTER 7

Tourists in London

Clutching the coin, Omar and I found a phone booth. I read the instructions carefully to make sure I did not lose the precious coin and dialled the number. There was no answer. I checked the time. It was just about six in the evening and it was cold. We huddled in the phone booth trying to keep warm as I tried the number every ten minutes or so. It was at that point that I vowed never to leave anybody stranded; that I would make it a point to always be present and waiting for anyone scheduled to arrive at any port or station. In the decades since then I have been true to that vow. At the time I was angry. This was the Dar situation all over again. However, thanks to Pam, we also had an address to go to. That would be our next move if we failed to make contact at that number.

Finally, at 6.45pm, the telephone was answered and I spoke to Vella Pillay. He told me he was expecting us and that we had to make our way to the Adelphi Hotel in Villiers Street near Trafalgar Square. A room had been booked, we should take the tube and he would see us in the morning. At that stage our money ran out and the call ended. What, we asked each other, is a tube?

We approached a policeman on the station concourse and asked for a tube. He pointed at the underground sign and we laughed. But we had no money and this transport was not free, so we walked out of the station with our suitcases. There were a group of men working on the road and we asked for directions to Trafalgar Square. A man I first thought was African directed us to a bus. His accent certainly was not African and I now realise he was from the West Indies. When we explained that we did not have any local currency and would walk to Trafalgar Square, he asked where we came from. South Africa, we said, and he immediately dipped into his pocket and handed us two three-penny coins. 'That will take you to Trafalgar Square,' he said, and pointed to a red double-decker bus.

The conductor motioned to us to get off when we got to Trafalgar Square and we asked around, found the hotel and checked in. The room was cold and we had no idea about heaters and how they worked. We were also tired and hungry, but our greatest need was to sleep. We dumped most of our clothing on the beds to act as extra blankets to keep us warm, climbed in and were asleep within minutes.

In the morning when we got up and looked around the room we saw that the heater had a coin box attached: no use to us without local money. But there were hot showers that helped to warm us up as we got dressed to wait for Vella Pillay. While we had been travelling we had used very few clothes, but we now needed to wash what we had used or we would run out of anything clean.

Such domestic concerns took a back seat when Vella arrived at about 9am, introduced himself and took us for breakfast at a café next to the hotel. We explained what had happened and that we were confused to find ourselves in this cold place. He apologised for the treatment we had received but said we should not worry, that we would be taken care of. He paid for scones and pots of tea before he led us to a building around the corner from the hotel and walked upstairs to a first-floor reception area.

Vella told us to wait while he went into another office. It was a bit like Dar, with us hearing talking, probably about us, and not being able to work out what was being said. About 40 minutes later we were ushered into the office by Vella and introduced to Dr Yusuf ('Doc') Dadoo, someone we knew a lot about because he had been president of the Youth Congress and was a leading figure in the liberation movement in South Africa.

Puffing on his pipe, he welcomed us warmly and surprised us by speaking about our fathers. He was aware that Omar had lost his father a few years before, and said he had been Omar's doctor in South Africa when Omar was young. He asked Omar about his health and he obviously knew the family well because he also asked about his mother and sisters. Then he turned to me and asked about my father and how he was. He said that when he had gone to organise the Indian community in Middleburg against the government, my father disagreed with his views, but they got on well.

Doc listened patiently as we relayed our experiences in Dar. We wanted answers. We hoped he could tell us why we were in London when most of the people were sent for training from Dar to other parts of Africa. This, we said, was why all our clothes were light and we were freezing. Also that we were only supposed to be away from home for six months and hoped to return soon to South Africa. Doc gave us no explanation, but assured us that he would speed up the process. However, he said we should relax because we deserved a break. He then enquired about Mosie, Paul, Babla and other members of the Youth Congress before advising us to take the opportunity to visit all the interesting places in London. We were going to be real tourists, but for how long we didn't know.

Doc said he would make a few phone calls and we should wait in the reception area. Perhaps we would get some idea of where we would eventually be going – and when. But when we were called back into the office we were only told that we had been checked out of the hotel and should go and fetch our bags and return to the office. Perhaps, at last, we were about to be told about our training. However, when we returned, Doc gave us each £10 and an additional £10 each to buy some warm clothes. He said we were to receive an allowance of £10 each week, which should cover our rent and our basic needs for as long as we stayed in London. We should call in to the office every Thursday to collect our allowances. He wished us well, adding that the receptionist would direct us to where we would be staying.

When Doc returned to his office, the receptionist gave us the address of the Harold Laski youth hostel and told us it was a bus ride away and near the Houses of Parliament. It was a bit of a whirlwind experience, but, for the first time since leaving home, Omar and I felt comfortable, relaxed and free from any pressure. As we were leaving I handed all my money to Omar. Throughout the trip he had looked after our cash and budgeted for both of us. I had also by then started the bad habit of smoking and he would keep me in check to ensure that I smoked only a limited number of cigarettes.

Finding the hostel was not difficult and we were met by the warden, who seemed very friendly and registered us before taking us on a tour of the premises. There was a common room with chairs and a television, something we were quite keen to experience. In the basement was a kitchen/dining area with all the cooking utensils and facilities. The sleeping quarters were basic: a long room housing 12 double bunk beds, six on each side. The centre area, we were informed, should be kept clear at all times and there were now 22 men in residence, so there was one bunk set free. I took the top bunk, Omar the lower.

We were also told that female occupants were housed on the first floor in smaller rooms. Between us there were two baths and a shower room and we should take care about the timing of our bathing and showering because the water took time to heat and there was not much available at any one time. The final instruction was that the shower and bath areas should be thoroughly cleaned after use, something we had always had others do for us. Even in Dar, where Omar had learned basic cookery skills, such cleaning was left to a servant.

Most of the information about the rules of the hostel we gleaned from the first roommate we met, who was from Sri Lanka and was intrigued about South Africa. He knew not only how the hostel functioned, but also where we should do our shopping. We took his advice and set off for our first experience of shopping for our basic necessities. It was an eye-opener, checking prices and deciding what to buy and in what quantities. As a result, we spent a lot of time walking around before finally settling for bread, milk, tea, butter, coffee and eggs. We also wanted meat, but did not know what was halaal or where to find it.

By the time we returned to the hostel it was late afternoon and there were many more people there, several of them clearly not what we thought of as youth. There was Jock from Edinburgh, who was about 40; Tony from 'up north', in his late 30s; Katherine, in her late 20s; a French girl, Jeanne; and 'Mr. Ward', who we assumed had to be 50. He seemed very aloof and very English and refused to shake our hands.

All these people had jobs – they were working on construction sites, in offices and in pubs. We got to know some of them quite well during our stay, along with a Labour Party MP who visited the hostel regularly. When he heard we were from South Africa, he took a personal interest in us. There were also, from time to time, travelling theatre folk, who only stayed for a few days before moving on.

But all that was later. Our first meal was eggs, bread and tea. We were quite anxious as Omar prepared the meal. Clearly, the kitchen and its utensils were not halaal, so we washed out the pan in which we cooked the eggs several times, since it was almost certain that bacon would have been cooked in it. We decided to buy ourselves a pan that we would keep for our exclusive use. We went off the next day and bought the pan and matching duffel coats, jerseys, socks and warm boots.

Completely kitted out, we still had a few pounds left over and went in search of a mosque. It took a while, but we finally found one. Unexpectedly, it was just a house and, by the time we got there, we had missed the afternoon prayers. What we soon discovered was that because it was London, and winter, prayer times were close together. And there was another realisation: Ramadan would soon start. However, at least we also got the address, in Soho, of the only halaal butcher shop, and Omar had learned something about cooking. But whenever we bought a chicken he insisted on stringing it up to keep it together before he put it in the pot, which I found very amusing.

Our story to everyone we met was still the same: we were on an extended holiday. And this we told Baboo Arif when we met him in London. We had been at school together, but had been no more than acquaintances and he had

London hostel life: Amin Cajee (second left) and Omar Moosa/Bhamjee (right) with two friends in London's Harold Laski hostel.

come to England to further his studies. He was lonely and homesick and soon became a regular visitor to the hostel, spending much of his free time with us.

There was also the regular weekly ritual of collecting our allowances and hoping to hear about when and where we would be heading for military training. By that stage we had come to address 'Doc' Dadoo as Mota, a term of respect and fondness that was used by most members of the Congress community. He was always welcoming and kept telling us that things were still 'being sorted out' and that we would be informed once all the arrangements had been finalised. Vella appeared to have disappeared from the scene.

It must have been fairly confusing for our families, because we continued to keep them posted about our travels, although we avoided mentioning how it was that we came to be in London or how we could possibly have afforded to get there. We also heard that there were people saying that London had been our destination in the first place; that the Mombasa visit had been no more than a cover for two young men who really wished to be in the Swinging Sixties capital. Those who thought this also seemed to be sure that we would stay in London for the foreseeable future. Our cover had been, if anything, strengthened.

We soon settled in and became part of the big hostel family, doing our bit towards the upkeep and maintenance. We also fasted and, whenever possible, would go to the mosque for the evening prayers. On one such occasion I found myself sitting next to the father of a friend and neighbour, Haroon, from Fordsburg. He looked surprised, said nothing and left. I did not think much of it.

Every Thursday, of course, we paid our visit to Mota and were always made welcome. The grand old man always made a point of sitting us down to discuss families, colleagues, what was happening at home and how we were managing. But it was still frustrating, although I think we were both starting to enjoy being tourists. Then, on one of our visits, when we had been in London for several weeks, Mota said that we should attend a party at the weekend. There we would meet many people, mainly young political activists from back home. He knew our cover story and said he was confident that we would handle ourselves well and not divulge any information. Besides, we realised, this would strengthen the notion that we were just innocents abroad.

Mota was right about many people from back home. I was quite surprised when we got to the party to see how many people I knew from school and from the Fordsburg neighbourhood. Many of them were from wealthy families who could afford to send their children abroad to study. All were men and, to my astonishment, among them were a number who used to ridicule us for our political activities and who, when at home, refused to have any form of association and contact with us.

Some of them seemed embarrassed at our presence and kept their distance, perhaps fearful that we would expose the positions they had really taken back home, which, in some cases, had been positively pro-apartheid. It was also obvious from some of the attitudes and questions we encountered that there was puzzlement about how we, from relatively impoverished families, could afford to get to, and stay in, London.

We soon realised that these so-called political parties provided an opportunity not only to socialise with what would now be called 'home boys', they also enabled these self-exiled young men to meet up with local female political activists from the anti-apartheid movement. I was also concerned that a few of these people might be passing on information to South African security. Fortunately, most of the chat was superficial and we informed those we spoke to that we were in London for just a short while and would soon be returning. After about an hour we left, both intent on not making another appearance at such a gathering.

The areas frequented by the partygoers did not seem to include the Laski hostel, where we remained to celebrate Eid, Christmas and New Year. This was certainly not military training, but we were gaining experience. And being in London was preferable to being stuck in Dar, apparently under suspicion and in an almost hostile environment.

There were constant comings and goings at the hostel and, over the festive season, we had new intakes from Germany. A whole group of us arranged to go to Trafalgar Square for the traditional midnight countdown to the New Year. There, despite the bracingly cold weather, we were amazed to see some people celebrating by splashing about in the fountains on the square.

It got still colder and by late January and early February 1963 the newspapers reported that we were experiencing the worst weather in 30 years. Then it snowed and snowed. For a week most transport was at a standstill; we had to clear nearly a metre of snow from the hostel doorway and the path. There was nothing to do but to stay in for most of the week. All I looked forward to every day was a hot shower and going early to bed. Omar and I raided the storeroom for additional blankets and, at one point, I had about six of them double folded on my bed to keep me warm.

Omar's cooking was very basic and when he got a letter from his sister suggesting we visit one of his cousins, who had been living in London for years, we jumped at the chance of what we thought would be our first South African-style home-cooked meal in five months. We decided to arrive just before dinner time, when we would be certain to be invited to stay for the meal, so we turned up on the doorstep at about 5pm. Omar's cousin was home and she welcomed us in and offered us tea and biscuits.

A short while later, her husband came home. He and I had been in the same class at school for about a year. We shook hands and sat and chatted about home, London, the weather and how we planned soon to return to South Africa. In due course, the wife excused herself and went to the kitchen, raising our hopes of a hearty meal. But, after a while, she returned, sat and carried on chatting while her husband excused himself and went into the kitchen, returning after about 20 minutes. There was no invitation to dinner and it dawned on us that while we sat in their lounge they were taking turns to eat their dinner in the kitchen. At seven o'clock I stood up and said thank you for the tea, and we left. This experience is, to this day, still fresh in my memory and has ensured that none of my visitors has ever faced a similar situation.

By mid-February the weather had improved slightly, but there was still no news when we made our weekly visit to collect our allowance. It was only the second time in all those weeks that Mota was not in and we were informed that he was out of the country for two weeks. We asked about Vella, since we had not seen him since the first day he took us to Mota's office. The receptionist replied that he was 'out' as well. Clearly that was all the information we were going to get.

As we left the office and were strolling down the street I suddenly felt that we were being followed and I mentioned this to Omar. He laughed it off, saying it was my imagination. But I was worried and told him that if we had been exposed, it must have been one of those chaps at the party who was working for the South African security service. Concerned that our cover was blown, I was unsettled for the rest of the day. However, Omar played the whole episode down and by the evening I was back to normal.

Omar had become very friendly with the Labour MP, who also served on the board of the hostel and frequently stayed over. He was very interested in us as South Africans and we invariably spoke about apartheid and the situation back home. He asked us why we were in London, not employed, and how we were funding our visit. We made up stories to cover ourselves and I am sure he was not convinced. Then one day he sat down with both of us and told us how he had helped many people from Southern Africa. If we were interested, he could arrange with an organisation to offer us scholarships to study further. We were taken aback, not at all prepared for this. We looked at one another and I said we would need to think about it and would let him know.

A few days later we received a call from Mota. He was back in London and wanted us to come to see him the following day. We were excited. This could mean only one thing: we would finally be on our way to do what we had left South Africa for. We were up early, had a hasty breakfast and, it being a fine day, decided to walk to the office to get there before 10am.

As we were climbing up the narrow stairway there was someone coming down and I stepped aside to make room. I immediately recognised one of the sons of a wealthy family from our Fordsburg neighbourhood who had been hostile to our political activities. He was the older brother of my friend Haroon, whose father had left the mosque so abruptly, and his family and ours had a very acrimonious history. He glared at me as he passed and rushed out of the building.

The hostility in that glare was not surprising given the relationship of our families, ours being poorer and working class and they seeing themselves as very much above us. One of my older brothers, Chota, and a daughter of this very class-conscious family had become romantically involved. This was unacceptable to the wealthy family and, when they found out about the relationship, they packed their daughter off to the UK. However, unknown to the family, the couple had been secretly married under Islamic law and she was pregnant.

Chota then followed his wife to London, where he faced claims that he had attempted to kidnap her. Lawyers were involved. Chota later successfully sued a newspaper for publishing the kidnap allegations and a legal agreement was eventually brokered. Chota would divorce his wife and, since custody of children in those days was invariably given to the mother, Chota acknowledged that the child could be raised by the wealthy family.

However, when the child, a son, was born, he was put up for adoption and there were public denials that there had been any birth. This was the bitter, class-ridden background. It was only in 1990, when I received a call from Wakefield Social Services, that the final chapter played itself out. I was asked if I was willing to meet my nephew, Mark Watson, who had been given away for adoption. He had traced me as the closest relative living in Britain. As Chota's son he was immediately accepted as a member of the Cajee family. Subsequently, at least one member of his mother's family also accepted him.

It should be no surprise, therefore, that that brief encounter rankled. When we entered Mota's office he greeted us warmly and asked if we had passed our Fordsburg neighbour on the way in. Apparently he had come to see Mota to find out why I was in London. His family, it seemed, had paid to have me followed and had traced me to Mota's office. I laughed and turned to Omar, pointing out that he had said it was my imagination when I said we were being followed.

CHAPTER 8

Czechoslovakia

Mota, who had been to Dar es Salaam, briefed us on his visit and introduced us to the convoluted ethnic and racial tensions that existed in what was a multi-national and not non-racial organisation. Omar and me turning up in Dar had apparently caused a lot of consternation because the major anti-apartheid movement was the Congress Alliance, comprising the ANC, the Indian Congress, the Coloured People's Congress and the COD (for whites). This apparently kept the African nationalists happy, while also being in line with the idea of separate 'nationalities' supported by the SACP. We, as 'Indians', should not be reporting to the 'African' ANC.

Our arrival in Britain resulted in the other congresses affiliated to the ANC requesting a meeting with the ANC National Executive to enquire what the policy should be regarding non-Africans in the military wing. We discovered that the two of us were among the first MK recruits classified as Indian, and perhaps the first to leave South Africa for training. We later heard that two other comrades of Indian origin had earlier been recruited in London and had been sent out from there and not through Africa.

This stress about differences was new to us. In South Africa, groups carrying out political acts came from all sections of society. In some areas, groups operated jointly. My brother Joe, Terry Bell and Mike Ngubeni, for example, operated a combined and short-lived group under the cover of the New Africa Youth Forum. We were all in the struggle together.

Because of this, we had been completely unaware that our arrival in Dar had created a major policy issue within the ANC external mission, led by Oliver Tambo. Without any consultation with leaders in South Africa and the rest of the external mission abroad, it seems a unilateral decision was taken that non-African members of MK were to become the responsibility of non-African exiled leaders. Recruits coming out should be referred to the relevant leaders abroad who must arrange the military training.

This confusion of multiracialism and non-racism created a major problem for a movement that was supposed to be fighting for freedom for all in South Africa. We were taken by complete surprise as Mota explained what had happened. If such a policy existed we might have apartheid in reverse, with 'Indians' perhaps being trained in India and Pakistan, 'Africans' in

Africa and so forth. Our arrival had apparently put the whole issue under the spotlight and, as a result, high-profile leaders from all the congresses had gathered in Dar to thrash out with the ANC the policy to be followed. According to Mota, the overwhelming majority supported the proposal that all recruits of any racial group coming out of South Africa should be the responsibility of the mission in Dar and be trained together.

Our minds were in a whirl as Mota completed his explanation. We immediately assumed that we would be returning to Dar to start again where we had begun. But it was not to be. In walked Vella Pillay, who, because he was concerned about the confusion regarding MK, had used his own contacts and arranged for us to go for our military training in Czechoslovakia.

We were to leave in two weeks and all the arrangements had been made. My first concern was that our passports should not be stamped by the immigration authorities in Czechoslovakia because this would jeopardise our legal return to South Africa. Perhaps arrangements could be made with the Indian government, that was sympathetic to our struggle, to stamp our passports to cover the period of our stay in Czechoslovakia? Vella assured us that this would be done. The ANC would take over full responsibility for us and would liaise directly with the Czech authorities. That was it.

The decision came as a shock to us. We were going to be trained in a communist country. Although we were aware that there were South African communists, including Mota, our vision of a communist country had been formed by the South African media and the apartheid regime.

The vision was of a country behind the Iron Curtain where awful things took place, a prison to which we were being sent. Although Mota and Vella had approved this venture, we were full of fear. We even considered then that the people in these countries might not be normal human beings. It was an irrational fear and we discussed what options might be open to us.

One approach was to go to Mota and tell him we were not happy to go to Czechoslovakia and ask whether it would not be possible for us to be sent to an African country for our training. What would his reaction be, considering how well we had been looked after? We also did not want to disappoint him. And what if he agreed with our suggestion and sent us to Dar? That thought, based on past experience, was enough to make the suggestion a non-starter. The offer of a scholarship suddenly looked very attractive. Perhaps we could just tell Mota we had changed our minds?

We weighed up the implications of this move. We were among the first non-Africans to be sent for training and we were thinking of deserting the struggle. What would be the reaction of Paul, Mugs and Blondie, the Indian community and the Youth Congress? And what of the effort that Mota and his colleagues made at the Dar conference for an integrated approach to the training of all? We also imagined that, if we did desert, this would probably give great pleasure to those individuals in the Dar office, and maybe even to Oliver Tambo. And to be really honest, we had got used to, and enjoyed, the life in London.

It was quite a wrestle with our consciences and we had to constantly remind ourselves why we had left South Africa in the first place. We would let down so many people by giving up. More than that, we would let ourselves down.

So we spent our last two weeks in London meeting up with the friends we had made and saying our goodbyes, informing them that we were returning to South Africa. When we met Mota and Vella for the last time they had a farewell lunch for us. Mota also gave us much-appreciated extra pocket money of £20 and, on 22 March 1963, about the time we should have been returning to South Africa, we left for Czechoslovakia.

We were both rather apprehensive about passing through British immigration and being challenged about travelling to a communist country on a South African passport, but there were no problems. Before we boarded our flight to Prague we posted our last postcards home. We would break off all communications for the time of our training, but this should only be, we thought, a matter of months. As it turned out, our families would have no contact with us for the next four years.

As we took our seats on the Czech Airlines plane our minds were gripped by all the propaganda about the communist bloc.

The plane taxied to a stop. It was late afternoon and it was some time before the doors opened and two men in plain clothes entered. They came directly to us, shook hands and motioned us to follow them. We were escorted off the plane before any other passengers. We had no idea how to respond: the reception had been friendly, but we were still fearful and the world outside seemed uniformly grey and cold.

As we walked to the baggage area we were asked for our passports and handed them over as we walked through various doors without once being stopped. We identified our bags and were then escorted to a restaurant for a snack and a drink. The men offered beer, which, as Muslims, we declined and, looking at the menu realised that, from a dietary point of view, it was going to be difficult from here on. We settled for a simple cheese sandwich.

As far as we knew, people in countries like Czechoslovakia had no idea of religion and we needed to set out some ground rules.

There was a brief discussion about our presence and our intentions in Czechoslovakia. We thought we would try our luck and, considering the two comrades knew little about us, set the agenda. We had often talked back home about the dream of becoming fighter pilots, so we went for it. It was a nice try.

Both the Czech officials were polite and told us not to worry. We were addressed as comrades Amin and Omar and we, in turn, reciprocated. I offered them cigarettes – Dunhill – and they accepted without hesitation. I was generous because I had 200 duty-free cigarettes that I knew would last me for a while. Besides, I was sure I would be able to buy more. Unfortunately, I did not realise that I was going to be stuck with a local brand for the rest of my stay. And that was going to be much longer than I had ever considered.

So our companions and I puffed on my cigarettes before we travelled from the airport in a chauffeur-driven black car to what we thought was a hotel. It was a week later, when we were moved out to a standard hotel, that we were informed that we had been staying in a special centre used to house members of the Communist Party who were in Prague from other parts of the country.

We were certainly well looked after, with a chauffeur-driven car taking us sightseeing. We also attended, as special guests, a military parade in celebration of the liberation of Czechoslovakia. Taking our seats we realised that we were in the VIP section for diplomats and foreign dignitaries. Fortunately, it was a street-level event so there was no offer of food or drink.

It was quite embarrassing at times to be treated like special guests. We seemed again to be on holiday. At no point were we questioned about who we were, where we came from or what our plans were. This surprised us and, after several days, we finally asked when our training would be discussed. Politely, we were told that matters were in hand. We were to enjoy Prague and not worry.

So tour Prague we did, escorted and chauffeur driven, and we were given the full history of that historic city. When walking in the streets or visiting tourist areas we noticed that we sometimes received stares from the people passing by, but this did not bother us because there were hardly any other people from Africa and Asia and I assumed that we were a unique sight.

Our fears and the views we held about communist countries were, we thought, obviously unfounded. While we did not meet or communicate with the ordinary people in the street, the environment was like that of any other city, with people going about their daily business, young people on their way to school, locals on their way to work. When there was an improvement in the weather we also managed to go out on our own and frequently visited a café on the embankment of the river, with the castle looming above. We relaxed and enjoyed ourselves in the pleasant surroundings.

It was in the second week that this idyll ended. We received a visitor to our hotel who introduced himself, in English, as Comrade Rudolph. This was the beginning of a relationship that was to last until the end of our stay in Czechoslovakia. He was very pleasant and ushered us down to a waiting car. We were taken for a full medical check-up, where the level of our ignorance was embarrassingly shown up. After various tests we were given vials to provide stool samples. We were disgusted and, in any event, at a loss as to how to proceed. Rudolph, amused by our ignorance, explained what we had to do during our early morning toilet visit. Further displaying our ignorance, we demanded to know what on earth would be done with the samples.

But the embarrassment was soon forgotten and we got on very well with Rudolph, who took us, during this period, for lunches and dinners to a restaurant called the Pelican. A few days after our medical he informed us that we were not equipped to be pilots because we were underweight and physically not fit enough. The second point was that there was limited time for our training, a matter which we had not considered. We were already well past our original six months and pilot training, Rudolph said, would take at least two years.

Rudolph then gave us our geography lesson: Czechoslovakia had three regions, he told us, Bohemia, where we were; Moravia; and Slovakia. We would be going to Brno, the capital city of Moravia; for our military training. A programme had been developed and all details would be provided on arrival. At last we were on our way.

We packed up our belongings, Rudolph escorted us to a car and we were driven to Brno. We arrived at the military academy in Krásné Pole on a late evening. There was not much activity to be seen, just blocks of buildings. With Rudolph guiding us, we entered one of the buildings, where we passed through a security room on the ground floor, and Rudolph informed us that we would be provided with security badges the following morning. Up on the first floor we were shown to a warm, neat room containing two beds with adjoining cupboards and to the clean communal toilets and showers. This was to be our home during our training.

We dropped our bags and Rudolph escorted us down to the huge dining hall, where there was a meal set out for the three of us. We had mentioned our dietary requirements, which had clearly been passed on, and we were presented with bread and eggs. But the main dish, as it was every day after that, usually contained either beef or chicken. So, for the first few weeks, Omar and I ate only the vegetables and really looked forward to occasions when dumplings and tomato salad were on the menu. Our diet was clearly not adequate and Khalek, a devout Syrian Muslim who always observed prayer times, persuaded us that, in the circumstances, it was okay to eat the meat.

Rudolph was a great companion. He spoke fluent English, kept up our spirits and gave us a tremendous amount of confidence. We discussed many topics with him – politics, literature, films, music, and sometimes sport. He was a major in the army and also spoke Spanish and French. He said he would be our team leader and we were free to approach him at any time about any matter. We were tired and decided to turn in early. Rudolph told us to take it easy; he would call on us in the morning. Once we got to our room and went to bed there seemed to be a lot of movement in the building, with raised voices at times, but we just ignored it. I must have fallen asleep the moment my head hit the pillow.

We woke early next morning and in the shower and toilet area made our first contact with the people we were sharing the building with. They were all foreigners of non-European nationalities, which surprised us. Rudolph arrived and accompanied us to the dining hall, where we found about 200 men in uniform, all of them apparently foreign. They seemed surprised to see us and we were certainly surprised to see them.

Still dressed in our civilian clothes we stood out from the rest of the crowd and were led to a table separate from the others. As we sat down to breakfast Rudolph explained that there was a battalion of Afghans and Syrians in the academy, sent by their governments for military training. This was good news for us, since both Afghanistan and Syria were Muslim countries and we assumed some arrangements must have been made for a halaal diet. However, to our disappointment, this was not the case. The only restriction was that no pork was served, but the beef and chicken were not halaal.

After a breakfast of cereal and scrambled eggs with toast and tea we were given a tour of the camp. Our accommodation block was a four-storey building with the Syrians housed on the ground and first floors and the Afghan soldiers on the third and fourth floors. There was also a two-storey administration building where officers had their offices and a third building that housed classrooms. The outer area comprised a number of sheds housing technical workshops. We were led to an office in the accommodation building and were issued two sets of winter uniforms and two sets for the summer, tracksuits, boots, ties, hats and trainers. Then on to the laundry room to be briefed on the process of submitting and collecting clothes.

We returned to our room to change into our winter uniforms and amused ourselves in a childish way by making comments about our uniformed appearance. Rudolph came into the room in his major's uniform, the first time we had seen him dressed that way. He had come to inspect the room and us, straightened our ties, although we did not think it really necessary, and took us to his office, down the hall from our room. There we were given a monthly stipend of 250 crowns, for which we signed receipts. We were also told that because it was a sensitive international issue we should not expose our nationality. No-one should know that South Africans from the liberation movement were being trained in Czechoslovakia (we did not know it then, but Czechoslovakia still traded with South Africa and even had a stall at the main annual trade fair in Johannesburg). And so it was that we became, nominally, citizens of Tanganyika.

By the time our briefing was over we were ready to head off to lunch, but were instead directed to the administration block, where, led by Rudolph, we entered a smaller dining hall. Seated around were a number of generals, majors and captains. As we were introduced to this group of very high-profile military brass, each of the officers approached us, shook our hands and welcomed us. We were both overwhelmed, embarrassed and also rather proud. But no-one had prepared us for this and we were unsure how to respond. It seemed none of the officers spoke English, and Rudolph played the role of interpreter.

Initially there was an exchange of pleasantries and small talk. But then a man we later discovered was the highest-ranking general stood up and made a speech. He expressed delight at having us at the academy, wished us well for a successful struggle in South Africa and pledged close relations between our two countries. We raised our glasses and toasted – we with apple juice, they with champagne. The lunch lasted about two hours and, as it was obviously drawing to a close, Omar nudged me to say a few words. Very nervously I managed to string a few sentences together thanking them all and expressing the appreciation of the ANC for their contribution to our struggle. It was my very first public speech!

CHAPTER 9

Getting down to training

On our first weekend Rudolph took us into Brno and showed us around. Like Prague, it was an old city with a long history. What first impressed us was that when we got onto a tram there was no conductor. Coins for the fare were merely placed in a box. Rudolph told us that everybody had to be honest and pay their fare and that passengers boarding were aware that they were watched by other passengers. It was 'the people' who owned the transport service and ensured that honesty prevailed.

After that first weekend we were given our timetables for the different subjects. What stood out was the hours of political classes we had to attend – about 35% of the course. The rest of the course included small arms training, topography, use of explosives, anti-tank guns, howitzers, military strategy and tactics, and so on.

Our lecturer in politics was Comrade Rederer, who was a lovely, jolly, down-to-earth chap who made us feel comfortable. Although he did not smoke, he always had a packet of cigarettes and allowed us to smoke in the lecture room. He gave us his overview of all the socialist states in the Soviet sphere of influence and we were instructed in basic socialism, using the *Communist Manifesto* and various other writings by Marx, Engels and Lenin. The purpose, we gathered, was to recruit us into supporting communism and joining the SACP.

All our lectures were conducted through an interpreter and, for the lectures on Marxism, we had two interpreters, Captain Slavinsky and Lieutenant Tomoski. On occasion, Rudolph would fill in as an interpreter and that always made the class more interesting. The Afghans and Syrians could manage in Czech because they had spent the first six months learning the language since all the instruction manuals relating to arms supplied to these two governments were in Czech. As Rudolph explained, the language of the manuals would not be a barrier for them once they returned to their countries. This would also apply to future arms sales.

Three weeks into our course we were joined briefly by two representatives of the ANC, Raymond Mhlaba, who on his return to South Africa later that year was arrested with the whole national high command at Rivonia, and Joe Modise. They had come out to see what training facilities were being offered and, to my surprise, although they were leaders of the ANC, Rudolph put them into the same uniforms as us. I thought at the time that it might seem demeaning to them. But they did not object. Another high-profile reception was to be held, which we had to attend.

At one point during the visit Joe instructed me to polish his boots. I refused and looked at Raymond, who smiled and nodded his head, agreeing with my response. Modise was clearly not pleased and I think I felt the repercussions a few years later in Tanganyika. But we had some interesting discussions with Raymond, during which we raised the matter of our experiences in Dar. He said he was not aware of what had happened and we filled him in about the way we had come to Czechoslovakia. He was taken aback and hinted that he would check on why this had happened. During the one-week stay of the two ANC reps I did not warm to Joe, and the feeling was apparently mutual. However, Joe got on well with Omar, even suggesting that he would like Omar to marry his sister.

By that time we had started to mix and socialise with a number of our Syrian and Afghan colleagues. They had arrived months before us and had made contact with the local people, mainly the female population, and we were invited to join them. The initial contact was made through our common religion and we exchanged information about prayer times. Our regular, off-duty haunt was a restaurant called the Slavia. We had truly settled in.

Then, in the middle of May, we were told we had been moved into another, larger, room. We immediately went down the hall to ask Rudolph about it, but he was not in his office and we were told that he had suddenly had to leave for Prague. It was a puzzle that we thought we had resolved when we checked out our new room: there were five beds.

This, combined with Rudolph having gone to Prague, seemed to mean that we were going to be joined by three more comrades from South Africa, something we looked forward to. But the way in which this had happened also made us aware that Rudolph was not as free with information as we thought. He was good at dropping surprises. Now I was coming to realise that we had to be on guard and not to take him for granted; this was the beginning of an education and awakening for me: don't take things at face value.

The three comrades who joined us were Gerald Lockman, nephew of Rivonia Trialist Walter Sisulu; Joseph Cotton, son of Moses Kotane, general secretary of the SACP and director of finance of the ANC; and Zelani Mkhonzo ('Zee').

Zelani Mkhonzo, who died in the Rhodesian incursions. Photograph given to Amin Cajee with the inscription: '...to a friend in deed and thought'.

We sat around for some time sizing each other up, not sure how to move forward. But we showed them around in the first few days and, at the weekend, we took them into the city. Soon enough we managed to gel. Zee and I became very close friends and I also became closer to Joe Cotton. Gerald was easygoing and very good at picking up languages, and he made friends locally and with a number of the Syrian and Afghan soldiers. Zee loved jazz and, in addition to our evenings at the Slavia, he and I would pop into the Continental Hotel, where there was jazz every Saturday evening.

The first time we went highlighted how naive we all were at the time. We ordered tea and sat listening to music. I noticed that Zee looked into the teapot and then sat back upright but did not pour his tea. I asked if he did not like tea. He stared at me and whispered that there was 'something' in the teapot. Carefully, I lifted the lid and saw a tea bag – something I had learned about in England – so I stirred the pot, remarking that there was nothing in it. Zee looked puzzled and pointed to the tea bag. He, like me in London, had never before seen a tea bag, and thought that it was some big insect. I told him about how I had first come across a tea bag in London and had reacted the same way. We had a good laugh.

But my outings with Zee became unpleasant at times because people would walk up to us and touch his hair or rub his face to see if the blackness would come off. Once at the swimming pool a number of young teen girls asked how often he bathed and when did he know he was dirty. They also asked if he had worn clothes for the first time when he came to their country and did he feel comfortable in them? Perhaps because the rest of us could be mistaken for Romanies (gypsies) we were spared these indignities. But it reached a stage when Zee refused to leave the academy. He stayed in for about three weeks and I became very concerned. Finally, all of us sat down and talked the problem through. We decided it was clear he and we were not the problem; we needed to go out and challenge this behaviour.

Zee finally agreed. Gerald, ever the linguist, had picked up a number of key words such as racist, stupid, ignorance and sick, and phrases such as 'how dare you?'. So, out we went as a group and the first person who approached and touched Zee's face we challenged as being racist and ignorant. This remained our tactic for all our outings. It was successful. We soon became known in the town, and also received support from some of our Syrian and Afghan colleagues.

To amuse ourselves, at times we went along with the stereotype and agreed that we lived in trees, that their ambassador occupied the highest tree in the jungle and that we had no dry-cleaners: all our cleaning was airlifted to Prague. Whether the satire worked, I don't know, but we would sometimes inform apparently gullible listeners that we protected ourselves from animals in the jungle with knives, not guns.

However, it was a problematic issue and one we raised with Rudolph and Comrade Rederer in our politics class. We asked about the level of politics taught in the Czech educational institutions. The ignorance we had encountered was among young people, a number of whom were university students. Their ignorance was shared by the older population, who seemed mainly to come from the working class. The official response was that this was the spillover from the old capitalist order and that the young were influenced by 'reactionary elements of the bourgeoisie'.

Because we felt that we were guests, we held back. In private, however, we rejected this oversimplification of the issue of racism. While we avoided confrontation, what had happened led me to examine the politics and the reality against the theoretical knowledge being fed to us. What was obvious was that concepts of socialism and communism were fed to the population through various centrally controlled channels of communication – the media, educational institutions, military establishments, worker and farming co-operatives – and on the shop floors.

But such propaganda from above did not seem to work. I discovered a decided lack of enthusiasm for socialist and communist ideology and way of life in many of the young people we met. Most seemed willing to give anything to migrate to a Western country.

It was the Beatles era and the youth were starved of every aspect of what the young generation in the West were enjoying. Literature, magazines, movies and theatre productions were restricted, or, in many cases, unavailable. The censorship was as extreme as that we experienced in South Africa. The only English newspaper available to us was the British Communist Party's *Daily Worker*, which provided the news when the national high command was arrested in Rivonia and where we also read of the death of Babla Saloojee and the imprisonment of Indres Naidoo, Shiresh Nanubhai and others.

We soon also became aware that there was a minority privileged class comprising members of the Communist Party and their families. They had access to what was called the Tuzex shop, which traded in goods produced in the West that could only be purchased with foreign currency. There were other privileges, too, which we sometimes enjoyed because Rudolph was a member of the Communist Party and held a party card. As a result, in his company we rarely joined a queue to get into an English film or a popular restaurant. Rudolph would bypass the line of waiting people, flash his card and gain us admission. We often felt guilty about using this advantage, but the occasional opportunity to indulge took priority over our principles.

This was also the period when Nikita Khrushchev was toppled from the leadership of the Soviet Union by Leonid Brezhnev. Comrade Rederer seemed to have some difficulty when we wanted to know what impact the changes might have, especially on the Soviet sphere of influence.

But while we were quite cynical about many of the claims made by our hosts, we had to admit that there were a number of very positive aspects to their system, such as free health care and education, the right of employment and the care provided for the elderly. We were also impressed by the support at the international level for countries fighting for independence in Southeast Asia and Africa. The elementary economics in our political lectures, about the treatment of the working class in capitalist and socialist societies, was also impressive, considering the exploitation we had experienced and knew of in South Africa.

But questions about any difficulties or failures in the economic strategy of a centrally planned economy for the whole of the Soviet bloc never really arose. However, we were aware that there was often a shortage of basic consumer goods in the local shops and an almost total absence of luxury items. This, we assumed, was the result of concentrating resources on heavy industrial production, with the Soviet Union dictating the terms. As we got to meet more locals we became aware that this had an impact on the morale of the population; on the fact that many did not seem to appreciate the advantages they had and why they, judging by their questions and guarded comments, apparently yearned to move to the West.

We were generally content with our lot, although our training focused on conventional, rather than guerrilla, warfare. We had reached a dangerous part of our training – learning how to defuse mines and unexploded live grenades – when we faced another problem. With no prior warning, three Kenyan cadets joined us in the academy. They were members of the Kenya People's Union, led by Oginga Odinga, the opposition to Jomo Kenyatta's Kenya African National Union.

The Czech officer who was responsible for them thought, like the others at the academy, that we had come from Tanganyika, so he introduced the Kenyans to us. It didn't take any time at all for them to realise that we were not from East Africa, let alone Tanganyika. But they played it cool and so did we, before rushing off to Rudolph to explain our dilemma. With his permission, we took these new colleagues into town to show them around and to explain our circumstances. They were sympathetic and agreed to keep our true identities to themselves.

All of us had training in small arms, all Soviet- and Czech-made weapons, and anti-tank grenade launchers, along with practical field training with 120mm and 57mm Howitzer guns and 57mm anti-tank guns. After shelling practices we were made to clean those huge guns and separate the shells from projectiles. We were also trained in driving T54 Soviet-built tanks, shooting stationary and moving targets, learning how to repair the tank tracks, drive heavy-duty military vehicles and jeeps in snow, and place chains on tyres in order to travel through mountain roads. This didn't seem to fit into the South African context, but we were told that it was all relevant.

There were, however, several minor mishaps during the training. The only gun I had ever used was a pellet gun, and when I was handed a rifle at the shooting range, I thought it would be the same as shooting with a pellet gun. I knew nothing about recoil and my first shot with the rifle left me in pain, with my shoulder bruised for a week.

The other notable incident was when Zee and I were instructed to use a grenade launcher. We were told to lie at a 45-degree angle to avoid the release of gases from the rear of the launcher. I was watching Zee as he fired and the expression on his face suddenly changed. He froze, his eyes wide. I asked what the matter was and he slowly moved his head to look back. My eyes followed his and I saw the side of his boot was missing. He just lay there as I rushed to remove the boot and saw a toe loosely hanging from his foot. He was in a lot of pain and was rushed to hospital, where the toe was sewn back on. His foot was just an inch inside the danger area.

For the most part, though, there were no mishaps, although the training was rigorous. We went out on a number of field trips for a week at a time in the forest, practising map reading, identifying areas for sabotage, and planning attacks and the ambush of enemy patrols. It was hard work and taxing, sleeping out in the forest in cold and rainy weather, although, at times, the weather was perfect. But we survived with minimum resources and comfort. On one such trip our supply vehicle did not turn up at the intended position and we had to track it for many miles, finally finding it after two days.

On one outing we were all dropped off during the day at various points and instructed to make our way to a meeting point 20km away through the forest, avoiding both villages and people. It was a good way of ensuring that we had taken on board our training in map reading and the use of a compass, as well as how to move undetected for long distances. All of this was supposed to be in preparation for a real situation in South Africa and we didn't initially think much about it. On that one occasion, four of us managed to reach the target area after what was a gruelling trek through harsh terrain. But, after two hours, Omar had not arrived and we trainees were concerned and discussed how to deal with the situation.

Rudolph saw this as ideal for role-play. He said we should think in terms of a real situation where we were planning an attack and an important link had been delayed. What should our assessment be? We decided to give it another 30 minutes before taking whatever action was necessary. According to Rudolph, Omar would approach the campsite from the west and we all stood looking in that direction, when all of a sudden we all heard a loud greeting coming from the east as Omar strolled in. Another lesson learned, as we burst out laughing with relief. Returning to Brno from our field trips was always a pleasure and we would head straight for a shower and a night out in town.

As the training progressed though, we became more and more concerned

TOP *Omar Bhamjee (second left) and Zelani Mkhonzo with two Kenyan friends, taken in Brno in Czechoslovakia during a break from military training.*

ABOVE *A long way from home: Amin Cajee and Zelani Mkhonzo knee-deep in snow in the Czech mountains during a break in one of their winter military exercises.*

about whether it was truly suitable for conditions in South Africa. We pointed this out to Rudolph, explaining that, back home, we came from urban areas and were more likely to be carrying out guerrilla warfare in that environment. Could he not see to it that our training programme was changed to suit our circumstances?

We were told that the conventional warfare training was all relevant, but Rudolph took the matter up with camp commanders and a number of specialists were consulted. They were older men who had, perhaps, been involved in the anti-Nazi underground during World War II. We were given extensive training in the components of industrially produced explosives and in making homemade explosives, and were made aware that it was possible to obtain various chemicals from pharmacists, agricultural outlets and similar commercial institutions without raising suspicion. In one lesson we were even taught how to obtain ammonia by scraping toilets and given practical lessons in producing homemade detonators. This became my specialist area.

We learned the importance of having a thorough knowledge of all areas of operation and of how to familiarise ourselves with the type of terrain suitable for guerrilla warfare. A lot of emphasis was placed on this and on the need to befriend local people and know the languages spoken in order to establish bases and build up caches of military and other supplies. We studied maps of South Africa, looking at what areas would meet the criteria for rural warfare. Our advisers concluded that a combination of rural and urban warfare was the way forward in South Africa.

There was a lot of discussion about how to infiltrate combatants into the country in small numbers, instead of large groups, and how to lie low and settle in, in order to create bases and establish means and lines of communication. It dawned on us that planning alone would take a number of years before we launched any form of attack, and the notion we once held about a quick, victorious struggle evaporated. Planning and patience were the key words stressed.

Our field trips also helped to prepare us for urban warfare conditions. As our training, including its special urban component, progressed, we were joined by three new MK recruits.

Without any warning, in December 1963 the three, bearing the pseudonyms 'Amin Jacobs' (Hussain Jacobs), 'George Driver' (James April) and 'Paul Peterson', arrived. Since I was already there as Amin, 'Amin Jacobs' became 'Ali'. 'Ali' was from Johannesburg and 'Paul' and 'George' were from Cape Town.

TOP LEFT MK *dude about town: Zelani Mkhonzo snapped by a Czech street photographer while on weekend leave from military training.*

TOP RIGHT *Demolition exercise: Amin Cajee listens to a Czech instructor as he prepares an explosive charge in a remote area of Czechoslovakia.*

ABOVE *Pictured in Czechoslovakia: Joe Cotton/Kotane (left), Amin Cajee and 'Paul Peterson' (Basil February).*

To my surprise, 'Ali' knew all about Omar and me. He knew my brother Joe and my family. When he was forced to go underground and had nowhere to go, Babla Saloojee had asked my brother to put him up temporarily. Until alternative accommodation was found for him, he slept in my bed. He updated me on the family and told me Joe was to marry Kamoo, who had seen me off in Durban. It was great to get all the news. He also said that the family was very worried because they had not heard from or about me for more than eight months.

As usual, we briefed the new arrivals on everything – the training, the politics and to be cautious of Rudolph. Zee got on well with 'Ali' and the three of us linked up because Omar had met a Czech woman, although they occasionally joined us. Joe Cotton, who used to be with me and Zee, linked up with 'George'and 'Paul'. Gerald was a loner who would join either group at various times and occasionally we would all go out altogether. This we regarded as our private time and what we said and did was our own business.

'Paul' was a member of the SACP and it was soon evident, especially in the politics lectures, that he was being groomed to lead the group. At the same time, Rudolph, with whom I had always enjoyed a good, although strictly professional, relationship, suddenly seemed to be aware of where we went and what we did during our time off. This created tension within the group and there were looming personality clashes. So I asked Comrade Rederer to discuss these problems. He complied and added a special period to the time-table during which we discussed our problems and this did seem to make a difference to the group relationship. However, by this time, Omar and I had completed most of the basic courses, while the others still had some way to go.

Towards the end of January 1964 Rudolph called us into his office. We had done well in our training and our results were outstanding, he said. We were ready to return to South Africa. We had been away from home for over two years and were all geared up to settle back and put to practical use our training for the struggle, confident that it had equipped us well to pursue our objective.

According to Rudolph we would leave for London within days. This was all too sudden and we were sad to leave, but the thought that, after a short stay in London, we would be back in South Africa was attractive.

For the next two days we were briefed to ensure that we took nothing with us that would link us to the academy. We were to leave behind all books and items that pointed to our training or our sojourn in Czechoslovakia. We understood and complied, knowing we had to make good our story that we had toured India and had therefore been out of touch for months.

CHAPTER 10

Cover blown ... and back to Prague

Rudolph accompanied us from the academy for an overnight stay in Prague, with the flight to London scheduled for the next day. We were handed our passports and, as I paged through mine, I noticed that there was no Indian stamp and no visitor's visa in it. I pointed that out to Omar and we realised that we had a problem. We would be arriving in London on a plane from Prague with South African passports that had no stamps to imply we had been in India, not in Czechoslovakia.

We went immediately to see Rudolph and explained our reluctance to travel without the Indian visa and stamp in our passports. He said he would look into it first thing in the morning and took our passports. We both had a sleepless night, being aware of the numerous glitches we had encountered on our way to Czechoslovakia.

The next morning at breakfast Omar and I were still concerned about the suggestion that we should fly to London without the appearance of having come from India. But Rudolph was nowhere to be seen. When he appeared he handed us back our passports, still without the Indian visas and stamps. He could give us no information, he said. He simply did not know what had happened, whether Dr Dadoo or Vella Pillay had been notified. There was also no information about who would meet us – or whether, indeed, we would be met. He was apologetic, but what could he say?

And so, with our stress levels high, Omar and I boarded the plane bound for London. During the flight all the feelings of insecurity and fear that I had experienced on the way to London the first time returned to haunt me. Before we boarded the flight we agreed that if we were confronted at immigration we would simply say that we had been given academic scholarships, but found the country unbearable and decided to abandon our studies and head for home. A feeling of doom hung over me as the aircraft touched down at Heathrow. Omar and I slowly disembarked and made our way, just as slowly, to the line before the immigration counters.

When our turn came, Omar went ahead and a few minutes later I went to the desk next to the one he was at. Omar was being questioned and, as I handed my passport to the immigration officer, he must have noticed that I was looking at the desk where Omar was. He paged through my passport looking for an exit stamp and I heard the officer at the next desk asking Omar a similar question. The game was up. 'Are you travelling together?' we were both asked and couldn't deny the fact.

The two immigration officers consulted and asked us to take seats as one of them left the desk, obviously to speak to someone senior. An hour later we were taken to collect our bags and ushered into a room where our luggage was thoroughly searched. We were then frisked and asked to remove all articles from our pockets.

What, they wanted to know, had we been doing in Czechoslovakia? We replied that we were hoping to study but were not happy and were now returning home, cutting our studies short. They told us that being South Africans we were not allowed to travel to any communist country and we had broken the law. However, this was not South Africa. We were in Britain, so I asked if we could phone a friend. They refused.

It was then that another man, obviously not from the immigration service, entered and began questioning us. It was clear that he was from British intelligence. But we stuck to our story and refused to give any further information. We were put under tremendous and, at times, hostile pressure, but we held our ground and were finally left alone, but only for about half an hour.

A different man then entered the room and the moment he opened his mouth his broad Afrikaans accent exposed him as being from either the South African embassy or a member of the apartheid state's external security mission. This confirmed to us how closely the British intelligence service worked with the apartheid regime. I still recall clearly his opening remarks: 'We are prepared to fly you to Johannesburg on our flight tonight and I promise nothing will happen to you.' He added that we could go back to our families; they would be informed of our arrival and would be there to meet us. I protested and said we were not willing to continue this conversation. We both demanded to speak to a British official.

The South African left and his British counterpart came in. I think a combination of fear and anger made me launch into an attack denouncing the now obviously close links with the apartheid regime. It was outrageous that the British had notified the South African embassy and I now wanted to telephone Dr Yusuf Dadoo, who lived in London. He would know what to do. At that, the Briton walked out and we were left alone again for about half an hour. Perhaps, I think we hoped, Mota would somehow rescue us, although our cover as far as South Africa was concerned was now blown. There was no way we could go back home legally.

The next time the door opened one of the immigration officers entered to tell us that we were being put on the next flight back to Prague. They were clearly concerned about the potential embarrassment about the links between the apartheid state and the embassy. But at least nothing worse was to happen, we were just heading back to Prague.

The whole episode, especially coming on top of our previous experiences, highlighted the incompetence on all sides when simple things such as a visa, and passing on information to London about our arrival, were not put in place. Somebody must have informed the authorities in Prague about our return because on our arrival Rudolph was waiting for us. He said he was due to leave for Brno the next day and so had been available to come to the airport. We were booked into a hotel and, as we reached our room, with Rudolph in tow, Omar and I turned on him. We were furious and wanted to know how such elementary slip-ups and incompetence could be tolerated. He just sat and took everything we threw at him.

The next day we were back at the academy, to the surprise of the South African group and others we knew. We had a meeting to explain what had happened and were listened to in complete silence. I think we were all rather shocked, and Omar and I were really depressed for that first week after our return. But we were put back into training in an advanced course. In our brief time away, the group – and its dynamics – had changed. In the first place, there were two new recruits, known as 'Stanley' (Abdul Satar Tayob) and 'Bobby' (Amin Kajee), both South African Indians who had decided to have pseudo English names.

They had travelled legally on passports in much the way Omar and I had and, when their training was finished, they were to return legally to South Africa via India. We sat around and had a good laugh, considering what had happened to Omar and me. But I did point out to Rudolph that he should make sure that when they left they should travel through India and not London. Using the racial classifications of South Africa, the group now comprised five Indians, three coloureds and two Africans. These differences did not matter to most of us, but 'Paul' made an issue about it and would refer to it at various times until 'Ali' challenged his statements as bordering on racism. Rudolph seemed, at times, to encourage these divisions and, on a number of occasions, I drew his attention to this and the effect his actions were having on the group.

There were other problems too. At one of the first political lectures attended by 'Stanley' and 'Bobby' we all soon realised that neither of the two was in any sense political. They had apparently had no real involvement in the movement in South Africa, but had been recruited by Salim Saleh, who was known to us and who we had met at meetings of the Indian Congress. We did not pursue the matter further and let them continue with their training at an elementary level. The rest of us were divided into two groups, with Zee, Gerald, Joe, Omar and me in the advanced group and 'Ali', 'George' and 'Paul' in group two.

Two months after 'Bobby' and 'Stanley'' arrived, 'Bobby' went into a fit of depression, and we took it in turns to be by his side. While I was spending time with him, he revealed that he was married and had a young daughter. He was missing his family and wished to return to South Africa. In the process, he explained how he came to be recruited. 'Stanley', who was his friend, had been forced by his father to marry a woman he did not wish to marry. However, the father had already agreed, deals had been struck, and a date for the wedding set. On the day, his father cornered him and marched him at gunpoint to the mosque for the Nikah, during which the marriage contract is signed.

A few weeks after the wedding 'Stanley' decided that the only way to escape was to leave the country, but he did not have the resources to do so. It was then that he heard whispers within the Indian community about recruitment going on for military training abroad. It seemed a way out, so he decided to join and contacted Salim Saleh because he knew that Salim was associated with the Congress movement. That accounted for 'Stanley', but what, I wondered, about 'Bobby'? 'How did you get recruited?' I asked.

What 'Bobby' told me, and 'Stanley' subsequently confirmed, was very worrying. It seemed that because 'Bobby' was a good friend, he simply de- cided to join 'Stanley' on what was portrayed as a great adventure. Neither of them, they readily admitted, had been involved in politics and nobody had explained to them the seriousness of what they were doing. Salim had not briefed them in any detail and they had had only one meeting, which primarily concerned arrangements for their departure. There was also no vetting procedure and, what surprised me most, was that when 'Bobby' and 'Stanley' reached Dar there was no security check. 'Bobby' said that they had had one short meeting with Jimmy, who was very friendly. They had stayed for a few days and were then put on a flight to Prague. This very different treatment from what we had received was apparently thanks to the intervention of Dr Dadoo.

The group gave me the task of monitoring his mental state, as 'Stanley' had simply abandoned him. Several of us took it in turns to watch over 'Bobby' and, after about a month, he stabilised. This, I think, was partly because of the promise that for both him and 'Stanley', training would be cut short and they would soon be returning to South Africa via India.

In the meantime we continued to train and also had holiday time off that we used to travel across the country, visiting Bratislava, the Tatra Mountains and, in what was a most emotional experience, Lidice, the town that was razed to the ground by the Nazis during World War II in retaliation for an attack on a German outpost in the town. Along the way we also called in on a number of glass factories and other industrial complexes, widening our experience and education.

In October 1964 Omar, Zee, Joe, Gerald and I were called into a meeting to review our training and to assess the level we had reached. We were told this was preparatory to setting out a timetable for a refresher period and to add any other training needs. All of us, we were told, had reached the rank of major, and we would leave for Tanzania in two weeks. There we would prepare for our incursion into South Africa.

At last the real thing was dawning. We were going home to join the struggle. We were all excited and Omar and I had no regrets, even though our scheduled and planned six-month excursion had turned into two years. In any event, after the London fiasco, we had resigned ourselves to having to return to the country illegally.

As soon as our briefing was over we rushed to tell the others the news. The excitement was catching for 'Bobby' in particular, who sensed that he would also soon be homeward bound. But there was no time for relaxation. Our lecturers put us through a series of crash courses to refresh our specialist areas. I was the lead officer for making homemade explosives and spent the last week going over the different formulae and making notes. Unlike when we left for London, this time we would be allowed to take with us all our notes and military journals. We were going home to join the fight.

It was another farewell tinged with sadness, much as it had been when Omar and I were packed off to London. We had made good friends with the Syrians and Afghans. In town there were a number of Czechs and Cubans with whom we swapped addresses and we also pledged to meet up again with the Kenyan comrades. It was quite a wrench having to say goodbye to 'Ali', 'Bobby', 'Paul', 'George' and 'Stanley'. Despite our differences we had grown close and were sure we would meet again at some point, all of us being involved in the same struggle, even if 'Stanley' and 'Bobby' seemed none too sure about it.

There was also some emotion in saying goodbye to Rudolph, Rederer and the crew who had trained us for all those months. It was again Rudolph who accompanied us to Prague airport. During our entire stay he had been polite and correct, but had shown no emotion. However, at the airport he took us by surprise when he shed some tears as he wished us well before we boarded a flight to Cairo.

This first leg of our journey was uneventful and we relaxed, having been told that we would be met in Cairo by the ANC representative in Egypt. Omar and I still had our South African passports and Zee, Joe and Gerald were using Tanzanian travel documents. No difficulties were expected with immigration. Once again, we were wrong. In the first place, there was no ANC representative to meet us and the immigration officials did not seem to know what to make of us. We tried to explain our situation and were taken to an interview room, where we produced our onward tickets to Dar on Egypt Air the next morning.

Check with the ANC office, we said, but nothing happened. Four hours went by before we were handed over to Egypt Air staff. Our passports and travel documents were held at the airport and we were taken into Cairo and put up at the Atlas Hotel for the night, given vouchers for dinner and break-fast, and told that we would be picked up next morning for our flight to Dar.

All went well. We all had a good meal, a good night's sleep and breakfast in the morning. The transport arrived on time and we were driven to the airport to board the plane. In sweltering heat at two in the afternoon the Air Egypt plane taxied to a stop. We disembarked and headed quite hap-pily to the immigration counter in a shaded building. We looked around for friendly faces. There were none.

CHAPTER 11

At last, Kongwa transit camp

When Omar and I presented our passports we were ushered to one side. Zee, Gerald and Joe, with their Tanzanian travel documents, were waved through. As they left, Zee called out, telling us not to worry, they would get the ANC representative to get us through. So we waited. Nearly eight hours later we were finally called and shown out of the immigration section, where Jimmy was waiting. He shook our hands, took our passports and walked us over to a car.

It wasn't a very long drive to the ANC camp just on the outskirts of Dar. It was dark when we pulled into the driveway of a house and we couldn't make out much. Clearly most of the occupants had gone to bed, but Zee was up waiting and had saved some food for us. We were really hungry and after we had eaten we were shown the bathroom to wash up, but it was pointed out that the toilet was located outside, about 20 metres from the house down a narrow path.

I needed to go, but there was no light. I stumbled down the path and, as my eyes got used to the gloom, I saw a square wooden base with a hole cut in the centre. Now came the problem: should I climb onto the base and squat or should I just sit on the base, not being sure of the condition it was in. To be safe, I climbed up on the base into a very uncomfortable position, cursing the fact that there was no light. Omar arrived with a torch, but it was too late.

At least we could see our way as we made it back to the house. We were shown a room with mats on the floor. In other circumstances it might have been uncomfortable, but we were exhausted. It didn't take long before we were fast asleep.

The next morning I was woken by Joe, who reminded me that we were back in a military camp and had a routine to follow. Omar and I were introduced to the other comrades, who looked surprised to see us, the only recruits they had seen of Indian origin. The camp commander introduced himself as Comrade Mampuru and welcomed us formally. He explained that there were a number of comrades who were housed temporarily in the camp. After being debriefed we would travel with them to the main transit camp, Kongwa.

Later that morning Omar and I were taken to the office and faced another shock: Jimmy told us to prepare for our legal return to South Africa using our passports. I was stunned and explained that it was impossible; that we could no longer travel on the passports. After hearing in detail about what had happened at Heathrow in December the previous year, he left the room to confer with someone. When he returned it was to tell us that no-one in Dar was aware of the incident. Bemused, we were driven back to the house. Zee, when he heard what had happened, was as surprised as I was. Communication did not seem to have improved.

The next day we were again taken to the office, where we were closely interrogated by Duma Nokwe, Moses Kotane and JB Marks[7] for an hour, during which we explained what had happened in London. As a result, we would have to be infiltrated into South Africa with other comrades. We again emphasised our desire to return to South Africa as soon as possible. We returned to the house/camp and cooled our heels for another day before being roused early next morning to bring all our belonging and get aboard a truck that would take us to Kongwa, some 240km from Dar.

The truck had a canvas canopy and thin mattresses on the floor to cushion us as we drove over the potholed roads. It was hot, dusty and uncomfortable, but fortunately not only Omar, but Zee, Joe and Gerald were aware of my problems with motion sickness. They saw to it that I was placed at the back of the truck so I could stick my head out of the canvas covering to do my thing. This sometimes made matters worse for me because when we hit potholes and the driver hit the brakes I tended to be thrown all over the place.

I realised with relief that we had reached Kongwa when, from my perch at the back of the truck, I noticed a sentry post with an unarmed sentry. It was late in the afternoon of 22 October 1964 when the truck came to a stop in front of a brick building, which I later discovered housed the administrative office, the sleeping quarters for the camp commanders and a large room that was the medical clinic.

I jumped out of the truck and looked around. There were another two similar buildings some 500 metres away and about 50 metres apart and, close to them, a line of five tents. The area, surrounded by bushes and knee-high grass, had been cleared. It was dry and dusty and near the tents I noticed four comrades lighting fires under two huge pots in what was obviously the open-air kitchen. About 200 metres behind the tents, in the distance, was what looked like a shed. It housed the communal pit toilet.

As we piled out of the truck, people started emerging from the buildings and the tents, and four comrades wearing plain green uniforms and caps approached us. We were probably all in our early 20s and they seemed older. It emerged that they were the camp leaders. They introduced themselves as Teacher, who was in charge of admin at Kongwa; camp commander Ambrose Makiwane; and Jack Gatieb and Archie Sibeko, his deputies. As we later heard, Teacher had been a teacher in a school back home, while Archie Sibeko had been a prominent trade unionist.

After a formal welcome 'on behalf of the people of South Africa', a phrase I was going to become very familiar with over the years, we were called to attention. By that time about 50 or more uniformed comrades had emerged from the tents and other buildings. Omar and I were conscious of the fact that we were being stared at and realised that we were the only Indians present.

Ambrose Makiwane addressed us, setting out the rules governing the camp, focusing on discipline. A lot of emphasis was placed on loyalty to the people of South Africa and the fact that everybody should follow the rules. There was no room for any disobedience against the command structure, and any form of challenge to the commanders would be seen not only as a challenge to the leadership, but as a challenge to the people of South Africa. This approach made me feel very uncomfortable. It was not the type of welcome I had expected, thinking I was joining a democratic organisation.

After we were dismissed a comrade was summoned to take us to the building at the end, where, as newcomers, we were allotted to various sections. Omar and I were split up. He, Joe and Zee were led to the tents, while Gerald and I were taken to the central building, in which four rooms housed 11 men sleeping on mats. We were shown two shower rooms at the rear of the building and told that the toilet was in the shed we had seen. We then had to take out only essentials from our suitcases, repack them and take them to the store in the adjoining building, where they would be kept. As I approached the storeroom I received a jovial welcome from an older comrade, who introduced himself as Victor. He embraced me and, for the first time since arriving in Dar, I started to relax. Victor was in charge of the storage room, where he also slept.

We were provided with two sets of green uniforms and a set of camouflage. I had wisely brought the footwear I had acquired from Czechoslovakia, which was clearly a better bet than what was on offer. We were also given two packets of cigarettes each: our allocation for a week. I was fortunate that Omar did not smoke, so if I did run short I could always turn to him to help me out.

I returned to the room and was introduced to some of the comrades with whom I would be sharing. Two of them – Steve, a muscular individual, and a man who went by the name of Jungle – stuck out as being very friendly. We immediately became acquainted and Steve, fondly known as Boetie (brother), briefed me on the routine in the camp. When the bugle sounded we all had to assemble in front of the building. This usually happened three times a day – early morning roll call, lunchtime and before the evening meal.

Steve had no sooner briefed me than the bugle sounded and we all proceeded to the assembly point. There were three platoons, each with three sections, each comprising ten or eleven comrades. This made up a company. The five of us – Omar, Joe Cotton, Gerald, Zee and me – who had arrived from Czechoslovakia were located in the three platoons and in different sections and were asked to come forward and be introduced to all the comrades. The other ten comrades who had accompanied us from Dar were returnees to Kongwa.

There was a section leader and the platoon commander, the person in charge, referred to as the 'man on duty', was responsible for bringing the company to assembly at the order of the camp commander. He was the liaison between the detachment and the commander or his deputy for the day. This position was to be rotated around all the comrades, and at the end of the last assembly the following day, 'man on duty' was announced and a process like the changing of the guard took place. The comrade known as Zola Bona (as Zola Skweyiya he was appointed as the South African High Commissioner to the United Kingdom in 2009) would then be requested to approach and would deliver the news of the day, which he compiled from listening to the BBC World Service, Voice of America, and so on.

We were then dismissed and made our way to the kitchen area. On that first day, as I walked toward the kitchen, I was joined by Omar and was surprised to see he was accompanied by a bearded comrade, Ahmed Xono, a Muslim brother, who was in his section. This heartened me and I felt an immediate warmth towards him. He had embraced Islam in South Africa and was involved with the ANC at home, which to me was unique, because back home the only African Muslims I had come across were the Muazin in mosques who called to prayer. This exposed my ignorance and Ahmed put the record straight, telling me there were many African Muslims in South Africa.

Another surprise was that he had first trained in Algeria and that when he had returned to Dar he had been sent to the Soviet Union for further training. I discovered that there were comrades who had trained in three different locations – Egypt, Algeria and the Soviet Union. Ahmed highlighted the problems with language with a story he related about a misunderstanding in Algeria where a comrade was being slapped by some Algerians. He kept shouting 'mercy, mercy' and, as French speakers, they continued to beat him, thinking he was making fun of them. Before our first meal, which comprised boiled cabbage and a fair-sized piece of meat with potatoes and gravy, Ahmed assured us that we could eat the meat because it was halaal. We had last eaten before leaving Dar and the meal tasted really good.

That first evening in Kongwa I sat with Omar and Ahmed and we were joined by Zee. I remember clearly that the sun was setting when I realised that I needed to visit the toilet. So did Zee. We walked to the shanty in the distance. Because the camp was still new, the path had not yet been established and the grass was sometimes knee-high. What about snakes? I thought. I turned to Zee, but he shrugged and, with a smile, noted that, as a fellow newcomer, he also did not have a clue.

Snakes, it turned out, were a reality, although we did not often see them. The only one I ever came close to happened to be in one of my boots. I was about to slip the boot on in the tent I was sharing with several comrades when I saw something moving inside it. I threw the boot out of the tent and as it landed, a snake, which we were convinced was a puff adder, wriggled out and into the grass. This led later to a light-hearted moment. It must have been about three in the morning when I rolled over in my sleep and woke up as my hand touched a long, cold thing. I shouted 'snake' and jumped up. This woke all the comrades and they quickly lit a lamp, only to expose my belt, which had fallen out of my trouser loops and was dangling above where I had been sleeping.

The path to the toilet was soon well worn with hardly any grass left. The toilet was constructed in a very similar way to the one in Dar: a wooden base with six holes cut out to accommodate six people and partitions providing a modicum of privacy. There were no buckets, just a deep hole in the ground. On that first visit with Zee we brought no paper and soon discovered that none was provided at the toilet. We backtracked and asked a comrade what we could do. He gave us some old pages of a newspaper and we rushed back. As I took a seat I became aware of the strong stench and I was about to bring up my dinner. Still, I did manage and realised that I had better adjust. After all, this, and far worse experiences, were what we could expect on the battlefield.

When we got back kerosene lamps lit up the camp area. I said my good-byes to Omar and went to my room. Most of the comrades were sitting on the bed mats and talking in a language I was not familiar with. My entrance caused a momentary silence, but, after a few welcoming nods, the conversation continued. I settled down next to Boetie, and soon became aware, from glances in my direction, that it seemed to be about me.

Boetie sensed my discomfort and whispered a translation: the conversation was about a white comrade who had trained with the Moscow group who, they said, had not lasted long. The last they had heard, he had gone to Europe. They wondered how long 'the Indian' would last. Through Boetie, I intervened and said that I had nowhere to go and that they were all stuck with me. This drew smiles and some laughter. By the time this little debate was over it was lights out time and I settled in for my first night in Kongwa, little realising how many nights lay ahead.

That first morning we were woken at 5.30am and the company was assembled for a run. It was a two-mile jog that at times picked up pace and I was having difficulty keeping up. I lagged behind the main group with other stragglers and heard a vehicle immediately to the rear. I turned around and saw the driver, but could not make out the passengers. As I continued running with the vehicle close behind me, one of the comrades whispered to me in English that the commanders did their 'runs' in a Land Rover. However, what captured my attention and really upset me was the sound of clinking glass: the commanders were drinking at that early hour of the morning.

After the run we washed and assembled for breakfast: a plate of maize meal porridge, a slice of bread, and tea or coffee. The commanders and the admin staff had their breakfast delivered by two comrades. Sitting and talking with a group of comrades I happened to mention the drinking in the Range Rover during our run. Zee asked if I was serious and I nodded. He shook his head and smiled.

Later, the company was assembled and we were marched to outside the admin building. The sun was hot and the temperature was already rising as we sat on the ground. After some time the commanders came out and we were called to stand to attention. One of the commanders spoke in English about our presence in Tanzania and our responsibility to the people of South Africa, who had delegated power to the commanders, so anything that transpired was all in the name and direction of the people of South Africa. At this early point I was getting a bit suspicious about this introduction. How could we claim to represent all the people of South Africa?

Many individuals did not speak English and, in an effort to ensure that the message reached all the different groups, the speech was translated into isiXhosa, isiZulu, Sesotho and, I think, Tshivenda, all of which took a long time. A speech that would have taken about 15 minutes in a single language took more than two hours. While I appreciated the need for the translation I kept thinking there must be a better way of getting the message across. I recall that my musings were brought to an abrupt halt with the introduction of Comrade Columbus, who had been charged with violating camp regulations. The case was presented and we were told it was up to the comrades in the company to pass judgement and decide on punishment – in the name of the people of South Africa.

The charge against Comrade Columbus was that he had left the camp area without permission. He was obviously guilty of this offence, but the suggested punishments shocked me: among them were 50 lashes, food denial for three days, and to be left in the sun for five hours without water. To my relief, a comrade stood up and said that a more suitable punishment would be for Comrade Columbus to run between the two end buildings for 15 minutes with a backpack filled with bricks. Sentence was passed and the company was dismissed.

CHAPTER 12

Kongwa and the 'people's court'

At the end of my first week in Kongwa we were allowed to venture into the local village, about half a mile from the camp. Omar, Zee and I followed some comrades who knew a shortcut through the fields instead of going on the road. The village had a single main road that was the centre of economic activity. There were five shops, most of them owned by people of Indian descent. The first was a pub run by a member of the Ismaili community; then there was a general dealership owned by a Hindu family called the Harmans; a furniture shop; another general store; and a teahouse run by a Somali man who supplied the camps with meat.

Omar and I became the centre of attraction as we walked through the village, being the only Indians from the ANC camp. Zee had gone off with another comrade and, as Omar and I passed Harmans, a huge Indian man waved and beckoned to us to come in. We entered the store and noticed a very attractive young woman sitting near the till with a small elderly woman. The man spoke Gujarati and Omar responded, causing the two women to burst out laughing. The reason, we soon discovered, was Omar's version of the language. According to Kumud, the attractive young woman, Omar spoke 'kitchen Gujarati'.

We were asked a number of questions and were offered tea and some Indian savoury biscuits. It was the start of a long friendship as the family adopted us during our stay in Kongwa and supplied us with food and spices brought up from their office in Dar. As they were Hindus there was no meat, but there were extremely tasty vegetable curries, dhal, rice and chapati. Sometimes there were also special treats such as sev or soji (sweet vermicelli and semolina puddings). Later they also provided us with a few small pots to enable us to cook in the camp.

Whenever we went to the village Mrs Harman had provisions – savouries and proper homemade vegetarian curries – parcelled up to take back with us. This hospitality was invaluable and something for which I will always be grateful. During these excursions we often found Jack coming out of the bar much the worse for wear and helped him into the transport that stopped close to the Harman store. We just accepted that Jack was an alcoholic and when we did our morning runs with the Land Rover following we expected to hear the clink of glasses.

Each section took turns to do the cooking. The section on duty would have to wake up early to prepare the breakfast, which was almost always soft mealie meal porridge, black tea and, if supplies had come from the village, some local bread. After washing out the huge pots, the section set out to prepare lunch, which was invariably soup made from whatever was available and cabbage. Always boiled cabbage. And bread. Then the duty section would have a break until late afternoon before getting down to peel whatever potatoes and onions were available, prepare the cabbage or, sometimes, *umngqusho* (a mixture of beans and maize kernels) served with meat and stiff maize porridge (mealie meal).

Throughout my stay in Kongwa, there was very little change in the menu and this led to comrades often going into the bush to hunt for birds or small animals to supplement their diet. If they were fortunate enough to kill anything the prey would be roasted.

Some months passed with the same dull routine. But the atmosphere in the camp was tense and I started to be careful about who I associated with and what I said. This was because, I think, most of us were aware that there were comrades in the camp who had been ordered to keep watch on others and who reported to the commanders. This made sense, since there was a lot of grumbling because we seemed to be going nowhere, doing nothing of merit. So a number of camp rules were flouted by a number of comrades, followed by the trials of the offenders and the constant reminder of the extreme and harsh penalties demanded by some comrades. The time these judicial processes took, with the translations into different languages, caused further strain and stretched the patience of comrades.

A few months after our arrival, and having obtained some spices from the Harman family, Omar wanted to go to Jack Gatieb, the camp commander, to ask if he could prepare curry for himself, Ahmed and me. I was a bit worried about this request and, out of solidarity, the three of us eventually approached Jack. He was all for it and instructed that we be given some meat for our use. So we had our curry. But a few days later Archie Sibeko ranted on about this deviation of ours and made a number of anti-Indian remarks. We were reminded that the revolution was 'purely an African one'. Okay, there were some non-Africans in the ranks, but they were being done a favour by being included. When the revolution was achieved the leadership would consider accepting Indians in the country. The Congress Alliance was moribund and the decision rested entirely with the Africans.

As with almost all of Archie's rants, this was in the vernacular and Ahmed, who spoke a number of African languages and translated what was said, laid an official complaint. Archie was called in by Jack and spoken to. However, to our surprise, the matter was not brought to the attention of our 'people's court'.

Other comrades, however, were regularly brought before this 'court' on petty issues that should have been resolved at section or platoon level; the whole process smacked of instilling fear, of the controlling authority exercising its power on the basis that this was in the name of the people of South Africa. Sometimes the charges almost descended to the level of farce. For example, a 'most serious' allegation against one comrade was that he had in his possession Chinese Communist Party periodicals. To my complete surprise – and to the surprise of many comrades in the camp – we were told that such publications were banned. Until then, most of us were unaware that there was censorship in the camp.

Comrades such as 'Pat' and 'Mntungwa', who had been trained in China, were often treated with scorn and mistrust. Anyone critical of the Soviet Union was branded a 'deviant Maoist and revisionist' or, alternatively, 'an imperialist tool'. We should all be on the lookout for 'fifth-column elements' that were against the liberation of South Africa. A number of comrades questioned this policy and wanted to know where it originated from and what other publications were banned. They wanted clarification of their understanding that the South African struggle was a national one which embraced people of all denominations and aspirations rolled into a single aim, the liberation of the country from oppression. Thus, there could be no one ideological norm.

According to Jack, the instructions had come from the national executive committee in Dar and the official policy of the ANC was to support the Soviet Union in the Sino-Soviet dispute. This was now official camp policy and all Chinese literature had to be handed over. Any violation of this rule would result in severe punishment. It was only later that I discovered that some comrades who had trained in China, as well as in Algeria and Egypt, where they had come into contact with Chinese material, had been sent to the Soviet Union for retraining.

The first group of 50, who established the base in Kongwa, had been trained at an academy in Moscow. The second group to arrive, numbering 70, were from Odessa. Our small detachment from Czechoslovakia came next, followed, in close succession, by groups that had been trained or sent for retraining in Odessa and Tashkent. Within weeks the camp housed more than 350 comrades, making up a complement of three companies and referred to as a detachment.

With the influx we had to clear more grassland to make way for additional tents to be pitched and we felt the pressure as numbers increased. Sections were reorganised, comrades were moved from the buildings to the tents and tempers flared when changes to the sections were made arbitrarily.

One comrade in my section refused to move from his room because he insisted that he had established connections with his ancestors in that room. Forcing him to move, he said, amounted to the ANC violating his beliefs. This, he contended, was contrary to the wishes of the people of South Africa, who placed a high value on this fundamental principle.

Eventually, the case was taken to the people's court to be resolved. To my surprise there was a lot of support for the comrade and his argument. It was a lesson for me to digest and it was reinforced as time passed and I became aware that there existed strong tribal beliefs among many of the comrades, among them some who professed to be communists. On many occasions they would tell me interesting stories of personal experiences or those of their parents and grandparents with spirits and how they had been in contact with those who had passed on. Such issues were not dealt with in the political lectures that were a regular feature in the camps, nor were they discussed at the various meetings that filled our days.

Among the newer arrivals were two female comrades, Rachel and Gladys, trained as nurses. When they arrived it was the major topic of conversation in the camp and they were assigned to the medical clinic, which was housed in the administration building.

Soon they both had partners – Rachel was with Dumi and Gladys with my Czech colleague, Joe Cotton. They were not officially allowed to live together, but, although their relationships were generally known about, they met discreetly and the commanders did not object. Many of us assumed this was because Joe was Moses Kotane's son and they couldn't object to Dumi's relationship with Rachel without involving Joe.

Leslie, who was from Natal and had worked at McCord Hospital in Durban, was put in charge of the clinic. He would walk around wearing a stethoscope and playing the role of a qualified doctor, although no-one was sure about his qualifications. Some comrades said he was a nurse, others that he was a porter. I liked Leslie because he knew Costa Gazidis, the doctor whom I had known and worked with in Johannesburg. However, my experience on one occasion in the clinic was enough to convince me not to return. I was ill and had a high temperature. When I was admitted to the clinic Leslie came in to take my temperature and pulse. He looked into my eyes and said: 'Comrade Amin, I am very sorry, but you have no pulse.' He then proceeded to fill a syringe in order to administer an injection. As ill as I was, I fled.

Despite some tension, I fell into the camp routine. Saturday nights were concert nights and a number of groups were formed to entertain everyone, the most famous being the Detachment Choir. There were no musical instruments, but the talent among the comrades was incredible. Some also made serious attempts to perform plays, but with only limited success, largely owing to the need to translate them into different languages. The same applied to a couple of apparently promising comedians in the making.

There was still no talk about where we should go from Kongwa and we were unable to practise our marksmanship because the Tanzanian authorities were not keen for us to be armed. While we were kept occupied with routine tasks and created other activities, we had a lot of spare time on our hands. As a result, small groups carried out activities such as hunting. But this failed to dampen the feelings of frustration. Nobody seemed to be planning our return to South Africa. At a leadership level it seemed as if there was no real urgency and we were given regular and often contradictory promises about how and when we would go home. Members of the national executive would come to Kongwa from time to time to give us pep talks, while promising that plans were well advanced to move 'the army to the front line'.

As the months went by, I became particularly friendly with a number of comrades. A small group of these new friends would join us whenever Ahmed and Omar, whose cooking had improved, managed to make a curry in the 'Harman pots'.

Many of us had been motivated by political commitment, but some had not been actively involved, including Oompie, who had volunteered when asked and ended up in Kongwa. Everyone seemed to have some knowledge of different aspects of what was going on, from the financing of the camps by the Organisation of African Unity (OAU), to the backgrounds of individual comrades they had known at home.

Discussing these matters helped me to understand the issues which started unravelling later within the camp. It also soon became clear that the ultimate control of such exile camps rested with the Tanzanians. Major Chikombele and Lieutenant Kilala from the Tanzanian army, who lived outside the camp, would pay regular visits and hold discussions with the camp commanders, a group that had apparently assumed control when the first of the trainees arrived.

The camp kept growing as more comrades came back from training abroad. One particular group of about 30 caught my attention. I was surprised to see that some of them seemed to be barely in their teens. They were apparently from Zeerust and I was told that they had all been promised further education in schools in independent Africa. Their leader, a 17-year-old and the only one of the group who spoke English, became part of the camp hierarchy.

I also discovered that discipline took strange forms. One example: when a commander walked towards the toilet we were called to attention as he passed by us. He would then raise his hand in salute, setting everyone in turn at ease. When he came out of the toilet the same procedure was followed. Anyone violating this practice would be brought before the 'people's court'.

This irritated many comrades, as did the sounding of a bugle at any time between 10pm and the early hours of the morning, rousing us to assemble in the dark. When this happened, we would invariably be given a political speech by commander Ambrose Makiwane, unsteady on his feet, having just returned from the village bar. The speech would be followed by the detachment having to sing revolutionary songs for anything up to two hours. But, at 5am, we still had to assemble for our jog over a couple of miles while Makiwane usually ordered the best cut of meat from the store to be roasted and sent to his tent. Makiwane was nicknamed Umbobo because of his frequent use of *umbobo* (a leather whip – a sjambok) to punish comrades who committed an offence.

Zola Zembe's name also derived from his favourite threat – he would warn comrades that if they misbehaved he would come down on them like a *zembe* (axe). The nicknames stuck and, when he later lived in England, initially as the SACTU representative, Archie Sibeko was still known as Zola Zembe.

I remember with horror the case of a 40-year-old comrade who was charged with and convicted of stealing the property of the People's Army (a blanket) and was sentenced to ten strokes. The majority of the comrades had pleaded for leniency, but the commander ordered the victim to be stripped and given the *umbobo*. At 7am, and in full view of the detachment, the offender was held down over a bench by four men, his pants were pulled down, and, instead of ten, the commander got carried away and administered over 25 strokes. Bleeding profusely, the victim was released and collapsed to the ground.

We were then called to attention and marched towards the kitchen for breakfast as if nothing unusual had happened. None of us said anything and there were no signs of disapproval. We were all aware that anyone who opposed or tried to mitigate the punishment would be labelled 'rebellious' and a 'doubted freedom fighter'. We were also aware that rebellious comrades were liable to receive midnight callers and be taken for interrogation.

Four months on, Joe Modise and a number of the ANC national executive members – Oliver Tambo, Moses Kotane, Moses Mabhida and Mzwai Piliso – visited the camp to confirm, officially, the leadership posts. Ambrose Makiwane was confirmed as camp commander, as were his deputies, Jack Gatieb and Zola. Chris Hani was named political commissar, Jojo chief of staff, Makopo logistics officer and Teacher was confirmed as administration officer.

The whole camp command structure, with the exception of the admin post, had been handed to isiXhosa speakers. This laid the foundation for a disaster from which the camp did not recover for some time. Because of the tensions and arguments among the leaders, the departure to Dar of Oliver Tambo and company was delayed for three days as a compromise was thrashed out.

As the talks went on behind closed doors for days and into the nights, information filtered out. It was said that Modise had reached an agreement with Tambo and the ANC executive. And so it was. The detachment was duly assembled and it was announced that Modise had been appointed Commander in Chief of MK, a position initially reserved for the president of the ANC and held by Tambo, who was acting ANC president. The camp command remained in place. This was obviously the compromise agreement reached: in exchange for the post of C-in-C, Joe had dropped his opposition to what he had earlier termed 'Xhosa dominance' in Kongwa.

Some in the camp speculated that Joe had been able to gain his position because he was, besides the very elderly John Motsabe, the only Setswana-speaking leader in an exile movement dominated by isiZulu and isiXhosa speakers. This was seen as important because the only direct infiltration route into South Africa was through Botswana, a Setswana-speaking country.

I was not particularly concerned about the announcement of the formalised camp structure because I was not affected. However, within hours, the whole atmosphere in Kongwa changed. Groups of comrades huddled together, often whispering conspiratorially. We, who spoke none of the vernacular languages, could only feel the growing tension. But some of the comrades explained what seemed to be happening.

There appeared to be two main groups, based roughly on language or tribal lines, with a third, less cohesive, grouping. Joe Modise had allies among members of this third group, who came mainly from Johannesburg and were largely Sesotho/Setswana-speaking. Moses Mabhida was regarded as the ultimate leader of the Natal (isiZulu-speaking) group, headed in the camp by Rubin, while Ambrose, Jack, Zola and Chris Hani, all isiXhosa speakers, were leading figures in the Cape group and looked to Oliver Tambo as their leader.

Prior to the announcement of the formal command positions, Joe Modise made frequent visits to the camp, where he contacted members of the Transvaal group to win support for himself. The camp command structure, he said then, alluding to the camp commander and the two deputies, was in favour of the Xhosas. This, he said, would have to change. During these early visits, although he was a senior leader from headquarters, he would be largely ignored by the commanders.

We were aware that what we were seeing amounted to a jockeying for position, both within the camp and within the ANC itself. With the original MK leadership all in jail, probably only OR Tambo and a handful of ANC and SACP leaders in exile held clearly defined and accepted positions. Given the situation, I suggested, for their own protection, that Omar and Ahmed, who had become very friendly and tended not to be involved in many of the discussions going on, distance themselves from our small group of effective outsiders, which included 'Mogorosi', Roy and 'Ali'.

'Pat' and 'Mntungwa', who remained very friendly with our group, usually informed us about what was said when Joe visited them in Kongwa. According to them, Modise had promised them roles in a future command structure if they supported him. He would raise the matter of camp command with Moses Kotane, Moses Mabhida and Mzwai Piliso and ask them to take it up with Tambo.

Additional information from the Natal group came through Karl and, despite the tensions, many of the comrades seemed oblivious to the power struggle that was underway. We outsiders, and some of the comrades being wooed by various groups, watched what was going on with wary interest.

There were almost constant discussions and 'Mogorosi', a friend who was well connected, mainly to comrades from the Transvaal, helped to enlighten me about the state of play. According to him, only about 60% of the Kongwa complement were political activists. Another group, which he put at 35%, comprised mainly young people who had been promised further education once they had completed military training. The remainder, he said, were individuals who were wanted for some or other criminal activity in South Africa. I bore this assessment in mind and, as I talked to more comrades and listened to comments made, it seemed that 'Mogorosi' was probably quite accurate in his breakdown of our camp population.

'Mogorosi' himself was no angel. He regaled us with tales of how he and Oompie had worked together at home. They had a scam going by which they would purchase furniture for a whole house, put down a small deposit and sign a hire purchase agreement identifying an empty property not belonging to them, to which the furniture was delivered.

Immediately after they had taken receipt of the delivery, their own truck would pull up and they would load up the furniture and deliver it to a pre-arranged buyer at half the original price. They were so successful, said 'Mogorosi', that they would even ask their customers to choose in advance the furniture to be delivered. I was never too sure whether it was political commitment or possible criminal prosecution that had driven 'Mogorosi' into exile. For Oompie, politics was a minor consideration.

Such revelations provided a rude awakening for me and Omar, as did the realisation that there existed such deep divisions filtering down from the top to every level in the camp. Omar and I had both integrated well and had bonded with our comrades. Although there may have been some initial wariness on both sides, we felt we were all part of one unit. But, as the distinctions at a language and tribal level became more marked, we felt increasingly alienated.

Even the idea of learning one of the vernacular languages seemed fraught: which one should we choose? We had picked up bits and pieces of various languages and there did seem to be a sort of patois developing among the comrades that blended the languages, including English and Afrikaans. We thought it best, as tensions rose, not to choose any one language over another, fearful that we might be identified with one or other of the groups vying for power. We decided to wait until the situation calmed down before we proceeded.

I was beginning to realise that I had perhaps been naive in thinking I had joined a movement that superseded all trivialities such as racism, tribalism, regionalism and ethnic groupings. In the camp this hope was being systematically destroyed by what can only be described as political pickpockets. These actions set the stage for the future of the movement. I think tribal, regional and ethnic differences and sentiments were exploited by individuals in leadership positions because unity at rank and file level might have confronted them with a force that would have exposed the hypocrisy and corruption that existed.

Tensions continued, although at a lower level, as more recruits returned from training. But the idea of returning home remained the major preoccupation of everybody, apparently from top to bottom. The problem was not just how we could get back home, but what we might do once we got there. And this related directly to the type of training we had received.

CHAPTER 13

The Czech contingent arrives

One late afternoon the ANC Land Rover entered the camp. As usual everyone waited in anticipation for a senior ANC leader to alight and bring us the good news that we were going to move south. To my total surprise, 'Ali', 'Paul' and 'George' stepped out of the vehicle. I called out to Omar and Zee, who were in the tent some distance away, and made my way to the Land Rover. 'Bobby' and 'Stanley' were not with the group and I was hoping that they had been sent through India, because neither would have survived Kongwa, since they lacked the political commitment and the stamina that implies.

We were all excited as we hugged and were eager to find out why they had arrived three months before their course ended. I asked about 'Bobby' and 'Stanley' and 'Ali' assured me that Rudolph had kept his promise to me to send them via India. After the usual reporting and camp formalities, 'Ali' was assigned to my platoon in a section different from mine. 'Paul' and 'George' were placed in other platoons further down the line. I introduced 'Ali' to Karl, our platoon commander, and to a number of comrades in his section with whom I had formed a close relationship.

After dinner Zee, Omar and I sat down with 'Ali', 'Paul' and 'George', who had settled in with their sections. 'Ali' informed us that there had been a complete breakdown in his relationship with Rudolph, which had reached a point where there was likely to be a physical confrontation. Later, speaking to me privately, 'Ali' said matters were made worse because, leading up to their abrupt departure, 'Paul' had inflamed the situation. This was the story 'Ali' told, and I decided not to ask 'Paul' or 'George' for their side, to avoid the Czech turmoil being dragged into the camp. 'Ali' settled into the camp routine and we shared the same associates.

I had also made links with many of the other comrades, including, importantly for me in later days, 'Van', who drove the Land Rover between Morogoro, Dar and Kongwa.

With new arrivals coming into the camp, including more female comrades, our number reached over 650. There was a lot of conjecture that the reason for the delay in moving south was to make sure first that all comrades sent for training returned and that serious plans were being made to move the whole army in one go.

Among the new arrivals were several individuals who were known to 'Pat' and 'Mntungwa'. They were comrades who held senior posts in the ANC internal mission and had been sent out of the country to investigate why there were no trained people returning to South Africa. They were mandated to return with people already trained or to bring back information about the reasons for the delay. They came at various intervals and all of them were sent for training and not returned to South Africa.

'Pat' explained that this was a real cause for concern because it appeared that there was either a breakdown in communications between Dar and the internal movement in South Africa or a deliberate attempt by the external mission to withhold information from the internal mission. For some reason which I did not understand at the time, both 'Pat' and 'Mntungwa' placed a lot of emphasis on this issue.

Joe Modise had not come back to the camp to make the changes he had promised in the command structure. 'Pat' and 'Mntungwa' were scathing about this, saying that Joe had never been political during the struggle in South Africa. According to them, his main role was to act as a bodyguard for Duma Nokwe. The atmosphere in the camp was increasingly poisonous, but the overriding concern was how and when we would be going home.

We finally reached a stage where it was decided to bring together representatives of the groups who had trained in different places on different programmes, to discuss and plan a strategy for the military struggle. We formed a discussion group, which was led by Zola Zembe, Chris Hani and Jack Gatieb and representatives from the Moscow, Odessa, Tashkent and Czech groups.

I was pleased to have Joe Cotton with me on this panel. But as the discussions progressed I was astonished to hear that the whole Soviet group had only been trained in conventional warfare; there had been no mention, let alone training, in any form of guerrilla struggle. Joe, too, was obviously concerned and agreed with my suggestion that he should introduce the issue of guerrilla warfare. The response was surprising.

We were told that there was no need for what Joe was proposing; that arrangements had been made for the Soviet Union to supply us with T54 tanks and heavy armour. The plan, it seemed, was for us to advance, in a conventional formation, through Botswana and into South Africa. My initial astonishment changed to fear. Both Joe and I pointed out that it was impossible to even contemplate a conventional confrontation with South Africa. We were listened to and, after a while, Hani acknowledged that we had a point. But then the discussion ended and no further meetings were arranged.

As we left the meeting I bumped into 'Pat' and 'Mntungwa' and explained what had happened. While they expressed amazement that such conventional warfare ideas persisted, they said they were not surprised. They had had a run-in over this issue with some of the Soviet military lecturers during their retraining and thought that, as a result, guerrilla training had been taken on board. But the debate had been opened up and it was strongly pursued. A group of us suggested that the commanders of Frelimo, MPLA, ZAPU and the South West Africa People's Organisation (SWAPO), who were already fighting in their respective countries, and who had camps in the Kongwa area, should be consulted, since they were well placed and qualified to give us direction.

The aim of our group – the four 'Czechs' and 'Pat' and 'Mntungwa' – was to retrain the commanders and all the comrades. We thought it essential that we move away from the idea of fighting a conventional war and look instead at protracted guerrilla warfare. As we went around explaining our position to the various groups in the camp, we were pleasantly surprised at the support we got. The so-called intellectual group, which included Chris Hani and 'Paul Peterson', who, we later discovered, were rising young stars in the SACP, were key to winning our argument. They readily accepted it because they tended to be well read on the subject of liberation movements in Algeria, Cuba, Vietnam and the struggles then going on in Africa. Their arguments for a change in tactics were usually much more eloquent than ours and were put across in all the languages in the camp.

When the commanders became aware that the strategy and tactics of the South African revolution had become a major issue they called a detachment meeting to stop the discussion, apparently on the basis that such matters should not concern the rank and file. They were clearly surprised at the reaction and quickly backed down.

It was agreed that a training programme would be established to cover the areas in which the Czech group, in particular, had been trained. However, we were also not to ignore conventional training as, it was argued, the struggle would reach a point where conventional warfare would be feasible. At this stage, both Chris Hani and 'Paul Peterson' stopped promoting the alternative view, apparently because it went against the SACP line.

In any event, there was a lot of other work to be done, what with the new intake. Much of the time was spent in constructing two buildings, one an armoury to store weapons, when and if the Tanzanian authorities allowed us to have them, and two additional rooms to cater for meetings. We were also instructed to build a small adjoining room for a purpose not identified. We assumed it would eventually be a toilet for commanders, but it turned out to be a cell to hold comrades alleged to have committed an offence. It was the room I was later to occupy.

The other construction site was much larger, a room 25 metres long and 7 metres wide, to serve as a kitchen area and dining hall. During the rainy season the whole camp area turned into a field of mud and this made all forms of activity difficult. A third large building the comrades named Da Nang, after the huge US military base in Vietnam. This building of permanent structures made some comrades suspicious. They openly worried that the transit camp was being readied for a long stay. So there was a fair amount of grumbling and we were all always on the lookout for some sign that some move was being made to move us out of Kongwa.

The grumbling persisted, but the buildings were completed and occupied and the routine carried on. Eventually it was my turn to be appointed comrade on duty. In this role I had to monitor the activities in the camp and work closely with and support the logistics section, which rotated on a weekly basis. Omar was put in charge of this section at the same time as I was appointed and five good comrades made up the team. We took our tasks very seriously.

I had no real interest in orders and supplies and this was the first time that I became aware of how orders were placed. Omar, who had, at one stage, worked in this area, brought to my attention a number of discrepancies. The two of us, with the five other members of our team, met to discuss this.

There was obviously something wrong and we decided not to involve anyone else at that stage. We would go back in the books for the past three months and see if what Omar had spotted was serious. So we got down to cross-checking the orders paid for and stock received. It was not a very difficult task since orders were placed every two weeks and, for example, we would use three 4-gallon (20 litres) containers of cooking oil in that period.

When we checked the orders for the previous months the books recorded that the camp was billed for eight 4-gallon containers every two weeks. In the three previous months we were also billed for 36 dozen toothbrushes on four separate dates. This item was especially surprising because when comrades requested a replacement toothbrush the request had to be sent to Dar for approval. As we cross-checked orders against deliveries we discovered every item we used – from sugar, salt, cigarettes and tinned milk to maize meal – had been double or even triple billed.

Four times the amount of flour, bread and soap used in the camp had been billed and paid for. I particularly recall one order for 40 tins of biscuits over a period of four weeks, which we had never seen. They were listed as being provided for some comrades who required 'a special diet'. Among other items nobody in Kongwa had seen were cold drinks, rice, towels, butter and eggs. The more we researched, the more worried we became. Having discovered a mass of corruption, we had no idea how to deal with it.

Who did we take this information to? It appeared that the camp commanders and the admin section were in it together. Perhaps we should take it to the Dar office? But how to get it there? And even if we could, who should we give it to? Eventually, taking all the documentary evidence, I called the team together for a private meeting with some of the older and more experienced comrades whom we trusted. We shared the information with them and requested suggestions about how to proceed. We knew as well as they did that this was a very sensitive area, because the OAU was paying the bills. The repercussions for the ANC could be serious if the information went public.

Over the next two days more evidence piled up as the team went further back through the order books. At the same time, we met privately so as not to alert anyone who might be involved in the corruption. We discovered that uniforms had been ordered, allegedly delivered, and had been paid for when we were all aware that our uniforms were donated by the Soviet Union – and there was a large supply in store. We could still not work out who within the camp leadership was, or had been, party to this corruption. However, what soon became clear was that the other party was the Asian businessman who ran the bar in town.

With the number of people involved I suppose that it was inevitable that news of what we were up to would leak. The story reached the other comrades and the next thing we knew, there was a call from some of them for a detachment meeting and for the commanders to explain what had happened. This triggered a lot of activity in the admin building. The team was called in and ordered to hand over all the documents: past and current invoices, order books and all notes relating to orders. We were then marched out, with orders to remain in our accommodation until further notice and not to communicate with anybody. Across the camp groups gathered, watching the team being escorted and placed under what one comrade referred to as 'tent arrest'.

A few hours passed and finally a detachment assembly was called and addressed by Zola Zembe. It has to be noted that on no occasion had I ever seen him drunk or taking a drink. Unlike the other commanders, he was rarely seen at the pub in the village, so it seemed appropriate for him to be addressing the detachment. However, his opening remarks were surprising. He said that there were rumours going around about corruption in the camp, yet there was no basis nor any evidence to support such allegations. He had checked all the relevant documents and could assure the comrades that all was well. Under these circumstances the matter was closed and no further mention would be tolerated.

The upshot was that the rotating system of oversight was abandoned and the commanders took over the day-to-day running of the camp. Our team estimated that, on average, the OAU was overbilled by 60%.

CHAPTER 14

Swelling biscuits and World War II

There was general awareness in the camp that news of the corruption allegations and what had transpired had been relayed to Joe Modise in Dar by Teacher, who was a close confidante of Joe. It was assumed that Joe had used the information to his advantage because, a week later, Ambrose was removed from the post of camp commander and we were marked and not very popular with the command structure or the Dar office. The plus of this, as we saw it, was that the corruption was discovered in the early days, about eight months after the camp was established, and might, therefore, be dealt with.

There was no further mention of this episode during my entire stay; we were never interviewed and no charges were brought against any of us or anyone else. Yet, daily, comrades were being punished for petty offences.

Perhaps, however, the information filtered through to the OAU because there was a reduction in the allocation of funds to all the camps and we had to make cuts in our food orders. Meat deliveries, which had been daily, were cut to three times a week and there was a period when there was a shortage of food and we were rationed. Faced with this and the reality that we seemed to be stuck in Kongwa for a very long time, comrades decided that we should grow our own food. This was fitted into our daily routine, the military aspect taking a backseat.

Within a few months, having taken matters into our own hands, we had a thriving agriculture programme, growing tomatoes, beans and maize, and a chicken farm to supplement our needs. This venture came to an abrupt end after the camp administration started boxing our products (including slaughtered chickens) and transporting them to Dar for the leadership. In protest, the comrades stopped working and the whole project came to an end.

Some were desperate for food. Snakes were hunted and wild warthogs were killed to supplement the food supply. At one stage a cat was included on the menu. I declined to eat it. Surprising skill was displayed by some comrades in using sticks to bring down birds to supplement their meals.

Living this way was affecting the health of many comrades, and the number of people demanding glasses (spectacles) increased by 30%. Some, we decided, were just interested in having them for show, but many needed them. Some comrades started having serious problems, complaining of severe stomach aches, persistent coughs and a range of other problems requiring medical attention. This meant that there was an increase in the numbers who were taken each week to the hospital in Dodoma for treatment. Within the camp there was a lot of discussion about our diet and the medical services available. These problems were raised with the commanders and we were promised that Dar was looking into the problems.

To make up for the shortages we complained of, Dar sent us supplies of tinned fish and meat from the Soviet Union, along with tins of dried biscuits. There was a huge consignment of these biscuits, which, although we didn't think much of them, provided some entertainment because, when immersed in tea, they would swell up to many times their size. We amused ourselves by competing to see whose biscuit would swell the most. One day a group of us were sitting around opening the tins of meat for our evening meal when one of the comrades found a date embossed on the tin: 1942! We were being sent leftovers of supplies from World War II.

This raised concerns about the health implications and certainly did nothing for the morale of the comrades. The matter was immediately brought to the attention of the camp commanders, but they were adamant that there was nothing wrong with the food. We should appreciate the efforts of the Soviet Union to supply us with material and moral support. And most important, if we were in the bush in South Africa and lacking supplies, we would be grateful for these.

Towards the end of 1965, when many of us had been in the camp for more than a year, the atmosphere was becoming increasingly tense and morale was declining. This was not helped by the fact that every few months or so we would receive visits from ANC leaders from Dar, apparently taking it in turns to try to raise our morale. It was always the same story: a lot of effort was being put into moving us south. Soon we would be heading home. But nothing materialised. At various intervals individuals would leave the camp and rumours would circulate that they were the advance guard, preparing for our move. But some would reappear a few months later and, apart from saying they had been sworn to secrecy, would disappoint us by telling us nothing.

During this period Major Chikombele called a joint assembly of all the comrades from the ANC, Frelimo, SWAPO and ZAPU camps. No details were given and about 2 000 of us assembled in ranks in a field outside our camp perimeter. The major and his colleague then drove up and helped an elderly woman out of their vehicle. The major informed us that the woman had been raped and that we were participating in an identity parade. The woman was escorted slowly through the columns, all standing to attention. She peered intently into each face as she walked past.

After about 20 minutes she came to our section and, on reaching me, she stopped. I froze as she stared and I heard whispered queries from the ranks behind me: 'Oh, Comrade Amin, what have you been up to?' Seeing my discomfort, the major smiled and moved the woman on. She had clearly been taken aback by the sight of an Indian in the ranks. Thankfully the assailant – he was not from our camp – was picked out and taken into custody.

Apart from that incident, life went on as it had, but then, in early 1966, Zee was informed that he would be leaving the camp. He said that he and George Mel, who had specialised in communications, were moving down south to set up a communications link. That was the last time I saw him. Later, information filtered through from comrades who had been in Lusaka at the time. They said Zee had managed to get into Botswana to set up a communications point, but that the ANC had lost contact with him during a raid of some sort. The Lusaka leadership was under the impression that he had been killed. We would find out later what had happened to George.

In fact, Zee had managed to avoid detection, secured employment, established himself in Botswana and was waiting to be contacted by the ANC. When, in early 1967, the ANC realised that he was well and safe, he was called to Zambia instead of being used undercover in Botswana. During what would be a catastrophic campaign in Rhodesia in 1967/68, he was in the front line in the communications section on the Rhodesian side and, according to reports that reached Zambia, he, together with his relief, Jimmy Duncan, was killed by Rhodesian forces.

After Zee and George had left, the situation in Kongwa deteriorated further. Morale was low and small groups were forming, discipline was waning and a number of people were starting to disappear after saying they would make their way south. It had been months since the last visit by any of the leadership and there was a widespread rumour that they had abandoned the camp. On a number of occasions comrades who had left to make their way south were caught, brought back to camp and placed into the holding cell and a long trial would begin.

As usual there were always extreme punishments suggested, ranging from the death penalty to 50 lashes or being deprived of food for a whole week. And, as usual, there were other, more sober, voices, seeking to find the root causes of the problems. Invariably, the reason for desertion was the desire to return home to fight. At this time, the moderates always got their way because most of the detachment was invariably sympathetic to the accused. Harsh punishment, especially for deserting in order to get back home to fight, would have been likely to cause a riot.

The commanders were well aware of the mood in the camp and so avoided extreme measures, especially since food and cigarettes had been drastically rationed. To supplement their rations comrades took to selling their clothes, or, if the opportunity presented itself, the clothes of others. This compounded the tension as shirts, trousers and shoes disappeared into the local population. Much of the income from such sales went to support the village distillery, which produced a very potent local brew called *pombe*. The local bar, selling commercial liquor, also did a roaring trade and cases of drunkenness increased in Kongwa.

So, while morale in the camp deteriorated steadily, the local economy, especially in terms of providing liquor, boomed. More establishments opened and prices fell, which seemed to result in even more drunkenness. Even on weekdays comrades would venture out of the camp without permission. Discipline was breaking down.

I was regularly assigned to sentry duty at night at the camp gate and would witness dead drunk comrades being carried back by their only half-sober fellows. As far as I was aware, none of the guards ever reported this to the commanders, hoping that the worst offenders would sleep it off and save us going through the farce of a trial and the unnecessary tensions it would raise. The amount of drinking and the nature of the local *pombe*, coupled with the poor diet, resulted in an increasing number of medical problems. What had once been a vibrant detachment with high morale was declining into a group of physically poor and frustrated individuals.

For some ailments some comrades turned to Comrade Biyela, who had learned traditional medicine skills in a village in Natal. One of his most popular remedies was for clearing out the bowel by using an enema and applying his potion, which he prepared from the local vegetation. He was such a pleasant and simple comrade and I must admit that, while I was cynical at first, some of his treatments were successful.

Although we were in different sections and platoons, 'Pat', 'Mntungwa', 'Ali', 'Mogorosi', Roy, Karl, Oompie and I met regularly to discuss the situation, analysing the problems and trying to seek solutions. One problem we identified was that politicians were controlling all aspects of the struggle. We considered that we were at a standstill because there was no military input. With the exception of a few members, the detachment in Kongwa was intact.

Clearly there had to be a reason for the delay in moving people further south.

We came to the conclusion that the ANC leadership had put political priorities above military strategy. The majority of members of the ANC executive were also members of the Communist Party and therefore politically aligned to the Soviet Union, and we believed that the close link between the Communist Party and the ANC had resulted in the ANC's pro-Soviet and anti-Chinese stance. As a result, the Soviet policy of peaceful co-existence with the West meant that, given the largely Soviet-supported and ongoing revolutionary struggles in Angola and Mozambique, the Soviets were resisting another confrontation with the West in Africa.

This seemed to explain the dire situation we were in and the stalling and lack of preparation for any form of military action against the South African regime. We wondered whose political priorities were dictating the role of the ANC and MK.

At this point I was, for the first time, made familiar with the composition of the Congress movement and the effect on it of the voluntary dissolution and subsequent banning of the Communist Party of South Africa. Our understanding was that after the banning, CPSA members had been recruited into the Congress movement and that many of them, who subsequently joined the SACP when it was reconstituted underground in 1953, were in senior positions within the different congresses. 'Pat' and 'Mntungwa' retraced their experiences within the ANC, taking into account that 'Pat' was once president of the ANC Youth League, following in the footsteps of Nelson Mandela, and 'Mntungwa' was a senior ANC branch officer. Their experiences and insights were a gift to me and my understanding of the workings of the organisation.

It also made me aware that I was sitting with two comrades who were also members of the SACP and who were now questioning their roles and the role of their party in what was supposed to be a national liberation struggle. There were discussions about the tensions and struggles being conducted by the nationalists and the communists and about the breakaway of Robert Mangaliso Sobukwe from the ANC to form the PAC.

These conversations took place at a time when many comrades were leaving the camp in frustration and, inevitably, being caught and returned. We were continually reminded that there was no escape and that wherever we chose to go we would be returned to face punishment. As we soon learnt, some of the comrades travelled successfully all the way through Tanzania and Zambia, only to be arrested close to the Rhodesian border.

The situation was becoming desperate and the leadership remained in Dar.

We had to wrestle the military objectives away from the political agenda. So we felt there was a need to try to get the leadership to Kongwa to address the issue in an open forum. In such a gathering we were confident that we would command a large majority to back the initiative to prioritise the military campaign.

The question then arose: what if we failed to persuade the leadership? What options would then be open to us? Some of the comrades suggested that if we had the backing of the overwhelming majority in the camp we could take direct action by detaining the leadership until we got results. Fortunately, that suggestion was quickly shelved when it was realised that such action would involve the host country's military and police. It would also be regarded as mutiny, a serious charge that we were not prepared to face.

In the midst of this ferment, the leadership sent JB Marks, Moses Mabhida and Joe Modise to Kongwa to announce that the movement was now ready to move people out. The logistics, we were told, were in place and there would be discussions with groups over the next few days. To my surprise, 'Ali' and I were called in by Joe Modise to discuss our role. He informed us that the movement had established contact with 'Stanley' and 'Bobby', who were safely and legally back in South Africa and operating above board. They would be our contacts on our arrival and were currently setting up safe houses.

As we spoke, Modise scribbled away on a pad, apparently making notes about our discussion. I had a chance to glance at these notes when he was briefly called out of the room by Teacher. There was nothing but meaningless scribbles on the paper. Not a single written word. When Joe returned to the room he cut the discussion short and said he would have another briefing with us and that we should bring Omar when next we met.

Although it was a very strange interview, our hopes were raised. It made sense that on our return we would be located in an Indian area and that would be our area of operation. On balance, we were delighted at the outcome and immediately told 'Pat' and 'Mntungwa', who had also been called in by Joe. In passing I mentioned to them that Joe pretended to be making notes, but all I could see were scribbles. They both laughed and said: 'He can't write.' I did not know how to react. 'Ali' just looked at them quizzically and asked if they were making up stories. Their response was a smile and a shrug. It was apparently a joke, but it was on us.

Overall, morale in the camp was given a tremendous boost. Joe had brought more supplies from Dar and we were all relaxed. Then, early one morning, Joe announced that he would be leaving with a number of comrades, among them the head of security. 'Ali' and I and Omar had not had the second promised briefing, but we excused that since Joe informed us that plans were moving so fast that he had to return to Dar for an urgent meeting.

Eagerly we waited as the days went by. Two months later, in August 1966, there was still no news and no movement of comrades out of the camp. We were back to where we were before Joe's sudden arrival and departure. The atmosphere became decidedly depressing, with tensions again developing among various groups.

Food and cigarettes were rationed and in short supply and this made matters worse, especially for smokers. Either singly or in small groups, we smokers would walk into the bush to be able to avoid being bothered by comrades begging for a puff. It was during one of these 'smoke walks' that I was made acutely aware of what seemed to be a dangerous development in the camp.

We had walked beyond the camp's perimeter and had settled down in the long grass for a quiet smoke when we heard voices approaching. We quickly stubbed out our cigarettes and hid them from sight: desperate comrades, we knew from experience, would follow you anywhere just to get a puff.

We were lying in the grass when three comrades from the camp passed within a few metres. One of them was talking in an intense and serious tone, but I had no idea what was being said because it was in what I was later told was isiXhosa. They strolled by, stopping at intervals, while we remained hidden and silent. When they were a fair distance away we got up and slowly made our way towards the camp. I thought nothing of this until I noticed that my two companions, who were walking behind me, seemed upset and were talking quietly but angrily in their own vernacular, isiZulu.

Something was clearly wrong and, as we neared the camp, I asked one of my companions what the matter was. He pointed out that the third person in the group that had passed us had been Chris Hani. Hani had been saying that as far as he was concerned there would be no role for the Zulus in a future government; that the Zulus might have a glowing yet overrated history with the likes of Shaka and Cetshwayo, but that it was time for the Xhosas to make history. The Xhosas would take control of the movement and the armed struggle.

I could not understand how Chris, a professed Marxist and member of the SACP, could reconcile these utterings with his ideological beliefs. So I went to 'Pat' and 'Mntungwa' and related the incident. They merely shrugged and said they were not surprised. We obviously had trouble brewing.

CHAPTER 15

'In the name of the people' – a death sentence

The trouble we feared arrived on a morning at the end of August and ended up with me in a cell facing the death sentence. It was the longest night of my life as I mulled over how I had got to where I was. I do recall that, once or twice, I heard Omar trying to get access to the cell and being turned away. As I thought about my life up to that point I also found myself reciting sections of the Quran that I had memorised as a little boy. This seemed to help, but did not wholly deaden the fear of the morning and of the pain I still felt from the recent beating.

As I waited for the inevitable sound of the key turning in the lock, I kept wondering where I had gone wrong. Should I have kept quiet and not made a contribution at the trial? Should I have chosen as my friends comrades other than 'Pat' and 'Mntungwa'? And what about exposing corruption in the supplies system? It might also have been a very bad move to have refused to polish Joe Modise's boots that time in Czechoslovakia. He almost certainly still held a grudge. These thoughts pressed in on me as the sun rose and it became slightly lighter in the cell. The camp was stirring. There were voices in the distance and the sounds of a truck and perhaps motorbikes.

Then I heard Joe Modise's voice. He seemed in high spirits and announced that it was already ten o'clock. Shortly after that the key turned in the lock, I was ordered up and escorted across the ground. I saw Major Chikombele, and he looked up and smiled, greeting me with a nod. This lifted my spirits – after all, this man was a fellow Muslim. I felt sure that he was not going to allow this lot to do what they wanted.

Nothing was said; he was apparently just checking to see if all was well with me before I was led across to the hall to face the panel. In spite of the major's nod and smile I was still apprehensive. The panel all sat silently, shuffling papers and looking stern. The body language alone was intimidating before the words were pronounced: 'Comrade, you have been found guilty of the charges ...' This was followed by a long and, I think, deliberate pause before I was told that 'after careful consideration' the death sentence was no longer an issue. I was to be put on probation for three months, during which my performance would be monitored.

The reason for this leniency, I was told, was because the panel had heard from Comrade Paul, who had convinced them that 'Ali' was a bad influence on me; that I had been misled over the years. Then came the stern warning: should the panel find me in breach of camp regulations or engaged in any activity contrary to the rules set by the leadership, they would not hesitate to reinstate the death penalty.

I wanted to make a statement, but was cut short and told I was not allowed to speak and should return immediately to my tent. I simply shook my head in the only form of defiance I could think of as I was escorted out.

Omar, who was waiting outside, walked with me towards my tent. Other comrades, who used to be friendly, avoided my eyes, some moving away, apparently fearful of association. When we reached the tent Ahmed Xono was waiting with tea and bread. It seemed that only Omar and Ahmed would openly be my companions until and unless the atmosphere in the camp changed.

The next morning started with much noise and shouting. We left the tents to see that some of the Natal group who had been involved in the protest, among them 'Pat', 'Mntungwa', 'Mogorosi' and 'Ali', were being taken away by Tanzanian military and police. Where to, nobody knew. But I was pleased to note that at least Karl and Rubin were still in the camp. Over the next few weeks, although I was kept under fairly constant observation, there were times when no-one was watching and I would get a warm embrace from the likes of Boetie, Paul Majwe, the elderly storeman, Victor, and other comrades.

As time went on and we fell back into the same routine, more and more comrades re-established their previous relationship with me. At the same time, news filtered through that the group that had been taken away was being held at Keko prison in Dar. News about what went on in various parts of the movement usually reached us through the drivers who ferried comrades and goods among the various bases. It appeared that the ANC leadership had asked the Tanzanian authorities to keep the four comrades they had taken away in prison for 'their own safety'. It was said that they would be targeted again if they returned to Kongwa and, because there was no other place to keep them secure, prison was the only option.

Such information, which could never be confirmed, trickled through mainly from Dar. But, apart from the comrades in prison, nothing had basically changed. We all soon realised that we were back at square one. As a

Socrates, also known as Maurice Mothombeni, whose given name was Abe Moloi.

result, a number of comrades left the camp and did not return. Most made it clear that they would try to make their way south. Some were picked up in various parts of the country and returned to the camp and put in the same cell where I had spent that long night. Invariably, they were punished, often by being lashed. And the old ways of the people's court were abandoned. The commanders took all the decisions about what punishments should be meted out.

The fact that the attackers who had administered the beatings and stabbings in the camp had included commanders was the cause of a lot of concern, especially since there had been no effort to have them account for their actions. Surely they could not have carried out something like that without authority and, if so, whose authority was it?

It was not until a new arrival, using the name Socrates, came from Morogoro to be based at Kongwa that I heard that the orders might have come from the very top. Socrates told me that he was in Morogoro when news of the attack on 'dissidents' had come through. OR was there, along with a group of comrades, including Socrates. Tambo, he said, laughed, stamped his feet and waved a stick in the air, obviously applauding what had happened. According to Socrates, this had had a negative impact on the morale of the comrades in Morogoro.

Three years later the ANC staged its Morogoro conference, triggered by an effective rebellion by a number of comrades led by Chris Hani. They had written a memorandum protesting about the 'nepotism and corruption' in the movement, the very things that had disillusioned so many of us in Kongwa. Some of these protesting comrades, including Hani, had been imprisoned in Botswana. When I received a copy of Tambo's closing address to the 1969 conference, I felt sure that Socrates had spoken the truth.

To a standing ovation, Tambo called for total loyalty and unity and called on his audience to:

Wage a relentless war against disrupters and defend the ANC ... Be vigilant, comrades ... Beware of the wedge driver, the man who creeps from ear to ear, carrying a full bag of wedges, driving them in between you and the next man, between a group and another, a man who goes round creating splits and divisions. Beware of the wedge driver, comrades. Watch this poisonous tongue.

Many of us knew that the seeds of the wedges were sown, cultured, cultivated and grown in the camp in Kongwa, where the strength and unity of the comrades, which superseded all trivialities such as tribalism, regionalism, racism and ethnic groupings was broken down and systematically destroyed.

The blind loyalty demanded by an unaccountable leadership was the effective instrument that broke up a united front of mainly dedicated fighters. The jockeying for power at leadership level encouraged an undercurrent of tribalism and ethnic rivalry. So I was not surprised that these issues arose at the 1969 conference or that they continue to this day. Nor was I surprised when I heard that Joe Modise had called for the death penalty for Chris for raising the issues.

Comrades who were labelled dissidents were those who had doubts and sometimes raised them about the competence of the leadership and, as the months and, for some, the years, went by, their numbers increased. Occasionally, however, a few comrades left on orders, apparently being moved south and, by July of 1966, there were rumours that the 'army' in Kongwa would be relocated to Zambia. But, as more weeks passed and nothing significant happened, frustration continued to mount. I was particularly concerned for 'Ali', 'Pat' and the group in prison. There seemed no way of getting information about them. Others were also concerned and some of the comrades had managed to get a message to Moses Mabhida, who might be able to visit Kongwa to brief us about the detainees.

In the midst of these concerns, in August 1966, I was called in by Jack Gatieb. He was surprisingly pleasant, asking me about my health, how I was managing and whether I needed anything. I was being very cautious, but there was no mention of the tribunal and the attack. The commander then offered me a seat and asked me about the possibility of giving the comrades lessons in making homemade bombs. I thought it over briefly and agreed. 'Good,' he said, and told me to make a list of the materials I would need. I did, but left the office not in the least confident that this would materialise. There was nothing close to a military nature taking place in the camp and perhaps, at best, this was just another activity someone in the command structure had thought of in order to give the impression that we were still serious about the struggle.

Three weeks after my meeting with Jack Gatiep, to my surprise, the commanders presented me with all the materials I had requested. In addition, they gave me a small storage facility with a lock and keys to house my supplies. My spirits were lifted and I prepared lessons and started the classes, deeply involved in my newfound interest. The first few weeks were all theory, split into five sections: safety, the initiator, the detonator, ingredients and the preparation of the explosives. I needed two interpreters to translate and it was hard work to balance the time. I could sense people becoming restless and irritable.

It was plain that a number of the comrades were extremely cynical about what I was doing. When I explained it to them they told me bluntly that all I would do would be to burn bits of things and this would never make an explosion. I suppose they also felt they were right as the course progressed, because, in the early weeks, I focused on the timing device for initiators.

Not being attached to a detonator and an explosive charge, all this did was create a spark and flames. For comrades trained in conventional warfare and used to rifles, bazookas, rockets and artillery, my demonstrations must have seemed a waste of time. For some reason there also remained a widespread belief that, when we reached South Africa, the Soviet Union would somehow supply us with 'proper explosives'. There would also be no time to prepare all that I was showing them, because we would be 'fighting at the front'. The mantra of conventional warfare ran deep.

Noting that it was not going well I raised the issue with Karl and Omar, telling them I would set off a major explosion to grab the interest of these comrades. They agreed that this should get the others to take me seriously, so I went off and prepared for my grand explosion. Just after lunch one afternoon I took about 70 comrades away from the camp and, with Omar and Karl assisting me, I went through the process, explaining in detail what I had prepared. Before setting off the charge I tried to ensure that the comrades were well behind a safety line I had determined. There was still a lack of interest and some scoffing from a number of them.

A few refused to move because they were not convinced that there was any danger or that there would be an explosion. When I insisted that I would not carry on with the demonstration until everyone was behind the lines, the cynics, some of them shaking their heads and chuckling, moved back. I placed the capsule on the initiator and tracked off behind the safety perimeter. The explosion was deafening. A huge metal block, which I had failed to remove from the immediate area, was thrown high into the air and a large number of the spectating comrades started running away towards the camp.

When the dust had settled there was complete silence, followed by applause as comrades moved towards what was now a large crater. As I was being congratulated and slapped on the back, pandemonium ensued: the camp commanders rushed to the scene and police from the village, with sirens blaring, roared into Kongwa, followed by Major Chikombele, his lieutenant and comrades from the nearby Frelimo, ZAPU, SWAPO and MPLA camps. They all thought there had been a South African attack.

I admit I was very pleased with myself. It had taken a long time, but at last, I thought, I had made my point about the training needed for the sort of struggle we intended, and needed, to wage.

CHAPTER 16

A deadly experiment

That quite dramatic exhibition meant that the point certainly got through to some people. A short while after my grand explosion, the Frelimo leader, Samora Machel, arrived with a group of his fighters, who joined my training sessions.

I did not repeat that first exercise and set off smaller charges, giving comrades practical experience, under close supervision, in how to carry out the exercise. I saw myself playing a part in demolishing the myth that our small army would fight a conventional war to destroy apartheid. Comrades with really useful training could be infiltrated back home to put real pressure on the regime.

For the first time in many months I, and I think a lot of the other comrades, thought we were finally on the right track and would soon be heading south. But once again it was not to be. Only a few weeks after the big explosion and the start of serious training sessions I received a terrible shock. I was walking towards my storeroom to prepare for a lesson that morning when Eric Manzie, our head of external and internal security, a Capetonian with whom I had become friendly, pulled me aside and, before rushing off, whispered that I should check all the gelatine capsules.

These capsules, which I filled with sulphuric acid, rested on a mixture that served as an initiator. This was attached to a detonator, which I primed into the explosive charge. The acid would take 90 seconds to burn through the capsule, initiating a flame and so setting off the detonator and the main explosive charge. The use of the capsules would give me sufficient time to move to a safe distance from the explosion.

I was confused and surprised by Eric's whispered warning, and it took a few minutes for the message to register. I entered the room and sat down. For ten minutes or so I did not move until finally I took the box of capsules and examined them. Each had been pierced with a pin, creating a hole. I did a quick test to check how long it would take for the acid to burn through to reach the initiator. I mixed a small quantity of initiator, opened the cap of a capsule, filled it with acid and placed it on the initiator. There was an immediate flame. I tried a few more with the same result. Had I used any of those capsules I would not have had time to reach safety. I, and whichever comrade accompanied me, would have been blown up.

I didn't know what to do. I couldn't make accusations that would almost certainly cause some sort of witch hunt and raise all the problems of the past. So I called in Karl and Omar and the storeman, Victor. I demonstrated with the capsules what had happened and they were unanimous in insisting that I abandon the lessons. I knew I could do that by requesting new supplies, which would take weeks to arrive, and I could then simply not restart the programme. But as I walked towards the administration block, I kept trying to work out who might have been responsible for the sabotage, especially since Eric Manzie, as ANC security, knew about it and had not acted other than to warn me secretly.

Whoever was behind this, I thought, must have protection and that did not bode well for me. So I approached Jack Gatiep and informed him that I had run out of capsules and a number of other supplies needed to continue the training. I would be unable to carry out any more practical lessons until new supplies arrived. He immediately said he would order what I requested. I thanked him and left, thinking that I had at least bought some time.

In fact, that was the end of my training programme, because, and to my relief, the supplies never arrived. I also had the opportunity to thank Eric, but although I asked how he had known about the sabotage, he refused to divulge any information. All he said was that I should be careful of my old enemies. On the following day, Eric left Kongwa.

Once again, there was no military activity in the camp and the trickle of people who left resumed. With morale low, hardly a week went by without one or two comrades absconding to try to make their way south or to Zambia to lodge complaints. Discipline had broken down and the only routine that remained was among a group that had taken it upon themselves to prepare meals from the limited supplies. Comrades would go to the nearby village at any time during the week to drink the potent local *gongwa* or *pembe* brew and would often return to camp, staggering drunk, defiant and refusing to accept any punishment. It was a sad state of affairs, with alcoholism on the increase. Some of my very close comrades and friends were among the group that seemed to have become addicted to liquor.

At that time my health took a bad turn. I was losing weight and spent most of my time sleeping in the clinic. During this period I had a visit from Boycie, who had been on the treason tribunal. He came to express his regrets about what had happened and told me he had changed his views about the leadership and about Joe Modise. He had come to realise that they had destroyed the struggle by also destroying a well-groomed army of liberation. Rachel and Jackie were very worried about my health; my weight had dropped to little more than 31kg and they asked the commander to get me proper treatment.

In January 1967 I was moved to the Dar transit camp to receive medical treatment. It was just two weeks short of two years since I had arrived for what I had assumed would be a short stay in the Kongwa camp before returning to the country I had left in November 1962, intent on joining the liberation struggle.

Two years on, Kongwa contained a demoralised army of men who were underfed and prone to malaria, diarrhoea, malnutrition, eye infections and depression. In the poor medical facilities all illnesses were treated alike, with medical supplies that consisted largely of painkillers, mercurochrome and purgatives. I had voiced my disquiet quite widely about the beatings, trials and brutal intimidation, along with forcing comrades to confess to being 'people's enemies, Trotskyites and Maoists'. It was also probably known to most of the comrades in Kongwa that I thought that sowing seeds of division on the basis of tribal, regional and provincial differences was criminal.

From the reception I received at the house in Dar that was the local 'camp', it was obvious that the Dar commander, the somewhat older Comrade Mampuru, and ten other comrades who were housed there, had been fully briefed about my views and activities in Kongwa. They seemed wary and most of them kept their distance, but I realised that if I wished to survive in this environment Comrade Mampuru was crucial. So I deliberately set out to win his favour by doing tasks for him.

Also there when I arrived were Mosie Moola and Abdulhay 'Charlie' Jassat, two of four detainees who had escaped from Marshall Square police station in Johannesburg by bribing a young policeman. Their escape, together with those of Harold Wolpe and Arthur Goldreich, made huge headlines because no political prisoners had, until then, succeeded in escaping.

Mosie worked in the ANC office in Dar and, because we had so much in common, this made my stay there more pleasant and I would look forward to his return every evening. We would discuss our families – he had married after I left South Africa and had two children who were at home, while his wife was in Zambia – and our social and political activities in South Africa. But when I raised current issues he was very non-committal.

Charlie was working at the ANC shop, the 'People's Bazaar', in Dar, selling fabric donated by the German Democratic Republic. He and his wife,

Harlene, had a home very close to the Keko prison. They seemed much keener than Mosie to discuss the situation in Kongwa and what was happening at the time. This I discovered after Mosie, one Sunday, requested a day release for the two of us to visit Charlie and Harlene. Mampuru, who, by that stage, had become quite friendly towards me, agreed.

This was my first unaccompanied day out. On my visits to the doctor I was always escorted by a loyal comrade to make sure I didn't come into contact with anyone. Charlie and Harlene lived in a block of flats and, given the sort of talk that had obviously gone on about me, I was apprehensive about the reception I would get. But I was very warmly welcomed by both and enjoyed the first home-cooked South African meal I had eaten in nearly five years. This became a regular outing and on some Sundays we met Harlene and Charlie at the home of a friend in town known as Shamshu, who was a clearing agent who helped the ANC to clear all their goods coming in from the Eastern bloc.

Throughout this time I kept in touch with Omar through the two-weekly inter-camp transport runs. 'Van', one of the drivers I had befriended, would bring in and take out letters. I was aware that the letters were probably opened and the contents read, but there was nothing contentious in our correspondence. On one occasion 'Van' surprised me by bringing a letter from my brother Joe. Like me, Joe had been recruited in Johannesburg by Paul Joseph and he, in turn, had recruited a cell that was linked both to a group in Soweto and to one in the white areas. Eventually he had left the country for Lusaka. It was my first contact with family in five years. 'Van' took my reply and that was the end of the correspondence. 'Van' told me that Joe had put an end to it.

Then, in February 1967, external ANC representatives, representatives of all the congresses, the SACP and its trade union offshoot, SACTU, descended on Dar from all over the world for a conference. Mosie told me that Mota was among them and had made an arrangement to see me. Here again was hope that I could bring about some change.

I was taken to the ANC office and greeted warmly by Mota. We went for a walk and I unburdened myself, giving chapter and verse about what had happened. For nearly two hours Mota listened without interrupting me. When, finally, I had had my say, he said he believed everything I had told him, but that, for my own safety, he would not raise any of the issues at the Dar meeting. He pointed out that if he went into the combined congress gathering and highlighted the problems I had raised, there would be instant agreement that investigations be launched. 'Then I will be back on my way to London and what do you think will happen to you?' he asked. It was a matter of personal safety.

He would take up all the issues 'in another forum' when there was some chance that influence could be brought to bear to address the problems in Kongwa. Obviously, there was going to be no quick fix, so I asked if there was anything he could do to get 'Ali' and the others released from prison. He promised to look into it. While I knew Mota was right about protecting me, I was not happy with the outcome.

So the congress meeting came and went and nothing seemed to change. I also made my weekly visits to Dr Parekh, a close friend of Mosie, Charlie and Harlene, who was fully aware of my position. We talked about the issues and he was taken aback at some of the things I mentioned.

On a medical level, Dr Parekh discovered that my problem with breathing, which had caused me many sleepless nights, was a blockage in the nasal passage caused when my nose was broken during the beating I took during the Kongwa attack. He arranged for me to have an operation and, over time, my health improved and I waited to be returned to Kongwa.

During this period Mampuru became very friendly. Because I had gone out of my way to be helpful, he was always doing me favours and giving me time off at weekends, which I spent with Charlie and Harlene. Japan, who was Mampuru's deputy, also became a close comrade. I worried about Japan because the lenses of his glasses were very thick and his eyesight was failing. But he insisted on riding a scooter in the Dar traffic. Within a year, he was involved in an accident and died.

In mid-March I was helping prepare lunch at the Dar camp when two of the top leaders, Mzwai Piliso and Mendi Msimang, walked in. Mzwai and Mendi were regular visitors to the camp, but never spoke to me. What discussions there were in my hearing were in the vernacular, so I was in the dark about what was being said. However, there were occasions when the word 'coolie' was mentioned and I realised I was probably the subject of the conversation. I ignored their arrival, but then I caught sight of 'Ali'. He was out of jail. Mzwai gave me a frosty look and I was not sure how to react to 'Ali'. I wanted to go up and hug him, but remained minding the pots on the stove. At least he was free.

CHAPTER 17

More corruption ... and worrying news

I was still in the kitchen an hour later and, when Mzwai and Mendi had left, 'Ali' came in and greeted me with a handshake, keeping his distance. I offered him some food and we went out into the yard and ate quietly. We started making small talk and he said he was surprised to see me as he thought I was in Kongwa, but was very glad I was in Dar because he dreaded being the outcast. With me there, he felt more comfortable. I asked about the others and he said they had also been released and split up between Kongwa and a camp in Morogoro. We sat in silence for some time. I did not know what 'Ali' was doing in Dar and, even if he knew, he was not saying.

Later that afternoon Mampuru called me into his room and sat me down to have a chat about 'Ali'. He said he was aware that we were very close friends and he was, therefore, going to put me in charge of 'Ali'. I was to report to him if I found 'Ali' engaging in any activities hostile to the ANC. I was stunned and initially thought he must be joking. How could I, a supposed fellow conspirator in a 'treason trial', be put 'in charge' of 'Ali'? But Mampuru was serious. So I took on the responsibility knowing well that there was no way that I would inform on 'Ali'. But it showed that I had Mampuru's confidence and he trusted me.

That evening Mosie was as surprised as I was to see 'Ali' and, over the next few weeks, we had many discussions about the events leading up to his imprisonment and the setup in Kongwa. 'Ali' talked about his experience in prison and the discussions he had had with 'Pat' and 'Mntungwa', their hunger strike, which did not last long due to the lack of support from the group, and how he had made friends with a local trade unionist who had been imprisoned for his union activities. At the time, the unions in Tanzania had a good underground and were opposed to the country's government.

The first Sunday after 'Ali' arrived I decided to be bold and approach Mampuru for permission to take him out with us to Charlie. He was apprehensive at first, but I managed to convince him, pointing out that 'Ali' was in my charge and there would be no problems. I was also concerned about how Charlie would react to 'Ali' because word had gone round that it was 'Ali' who was to blame for the blow-up in Czechoslovakia and for the Kongwa troubles.

I had already explained to Charlie that these events had nothing to do with 'Ali', but he was still concerned. However, 'Ali' was well received and, during our many outings, he built a strong bond with Charlie and Harlene, and we met a number of their local friends. There were also social gatherings with Dr Parekh and his family. He was aware of the problems at Kongwa and told us if we needed any help, we should call on him. On many occasions Charlie, Harlene and Dr Parekh would slip cash into our hands. We put this aside, although I would send some to Omar with one of the inter-camp drivers, 'Van' or Albert.

During one of our early outings with Charlie and Harlene I was shocked when Charlie collapsed. His body was rigid and he seemed to be in a trance, grinding his teeth. Harlene moved quickly. She asked me to remove my belt and she forced open Charlie's mouth and placed the belt between his teeth to prevent him from biting his tongue. It was a form of epilepsy, triggered, apparently, by the torture he had suffered in police custody in South Africa.

In late April Charlie had to fly to East Germany to get supplies for the shop. The office decided that there should be two people in the shop and I was called in by Mampuru and informed that, in Charlie's absence, I was to join the assistant, Comrade Nkula, there. To familiarise myself with the setup I started a week before Charlie left. But, as I told Charlie at the outset, I preferred not to be in charge of the till. I did not want to handle any cash and it was agreed that Nkula would take the money and give any change due.

In the first week after Charlie left I became aware that Comrade Nkula was taking cash out of the till. This was reflected in the fact that the daily takings were dropping. I monitored the sales for a few days and worked out that Nkula was under-recording the sales we made and pocketing the difference between the daily sales figure and the actual cash collected. This discovery really frightened me. I had avoided dealing with the till for this very reason: that I might be the victim if there was any shortfall. When I got back to the camp I discussed this with 'Ali'. At that stage, I had decided to quit the job, but could not think of a plausible reason.

I then decided to take the matter up with Mampuru. He was shocked, but we had no evidence, so we planned that when Nkula went into the shower every evening Mampuru would check how much cash he had in his pockets and keep a record over the next few days. This would give us an idea of how much he had been stealing from the till. Every evening Mampuru reported to me the amount of cash he had found in Nkula's pockets. By the fifth day there was more than 900 shillings and Mampuru spoke to Peter Dlamini, who had come in from Kongwa a few weeks before and was closely associated with the camp leadership. Mampuru showed him the money that had been confiscated and Peter reported the matter to Mendi and Mzwai.

Nkula was confronted and admitted the theft. He was moved to Morogoro, but no other action was taken and Japan and I were left running the shop. To protect myself as much as anything else, I instituted a monitoring system whereby we recorded all transactions on paper and, at the end of each day, checked the figures against the cash in the till. I thought I had done well, but I felt hostility from Mendi, and particularly from Mzwai Piliso, who had enjoyed a very close relationship with Nkula. It seemed that, once more, I had not made a popular move.

In early May Gerald Lockman joined us in Dar. He had escaped from Kongwa in March, but had been caught on the border with Zambia and had fallen ill. He had then lapsed into a depression and, being the nephew of Walter Sisulu, he was sent to Dar for specialist treatment at the local hospital. For the first few days Gerald would walk around the camp talking to himself and keeping his distance from everybody, not speaking and showing severe signs of apparent mental illness. 'Ali' and I were concerned because we had enjoyed a very good relationship with him in Czechoslovakia.

Gerald Lockman (Sisulu), the well-connected MK volunteer who feigned mental illness and eventually fled to Zambia where he married and became a businessman in Kitwe.

It must have been a week later that 'Ali' remarked to me that Gerald was faking his illness. I was upset and told him he was talking nonsense. The comrade was really ill. 'Ali' laughed and told me to watch carefully. He took me to where Gerald was sitting a distance away from the house and, as we walked towards him, he lowered his head and I noticed a smile as he lifted his head slightly and winked. He had been pulling this fake illness for at least two months and had even conned the doctors at the hospital.

It was late at night and very hot and 'Ali' and I were sitting outside in the dark when we heard a noise and became aware that someone was crouching behind us. It was Gerald. He informed us in a whisper that he was going to leave the next morning and make his way to Zambia. Gerald disappeared early in the morning and the alarm was sounded. Land Rovers and scooters were sent out to track him down and Mampuru and Peter questioned everyone in the camp. They all pleaded ignorance. We thought Gerald must have made contact with somebody during his visits to the hospital in order to make his escape. We just hoped that he would not be caught.

The following Saturday morning George Mel, a close friend of 'Ali', who had left Kongwa early in 1966 with Zee, made an unexpected visit from Morogoro. We were surprised to see him in Dar, especially since he was not unwell, and medical conditions were the usual reasons for relocating someone to Dar.

George took 'Ali' for a walk and they were out of sight of the house for about an hour. 'Ali' looked serious, which meant George had given him some important information. We were going out later to visit Charlie and Harlene, so we would have the opportunity to talk. 'Ali' was very quiet as we walked to the bus stop. Mosie was with us, so I thought there was no way he would reveal anything. When we reached Charlie's place we made an excuse to go for a walk.

The first words 'Ali' uttered were: 'We need to get out as soon as possible.' I stopped and looked at him, confused. What was he talking about? It seemed that George, who had used the need to get some radio parts from Dar as an excuse to visit 'Ali', had passed on information from meetings and transmissions between Morogoro and Lusaka that included discussions among several of the leaders of the movement, including Joe Modise, OR Tambo and Chris Hani.

It seemed that, for some time, the OAU had been frustrated with the ANC hanging about in Tanzania and Zambia, while the liberation movements in Mozambique, Angola, Rhodesia and even South West Africa were engaged in different levels of military activity in those countries. Alone among these movements, the ANC seemed idle. This was draining OAU resources and Tambo had been called to a number of meetings to report on what progress the ANC was making in South Africa. There was panic within the executive and Joe was under pressure to produce results.

Unknown to the comrades in Kongwa, there were also ongoing discussions about joint operations with ZAPU and its military wing, the Zimbabwe People's Revolutionary Army (ZIPRA), which also had the support of the Soviet Union. The Zimbabwe African National Union (ZANU) was backed by China. The ANC leadership, together with Joe Modise, had selected a number of people to look into the feasibility of joint operations with ZIPRA. When this became public knowledge among comrades in Lusaka, many of them labelled it as preposterous from a military perspective. It would serve only to provide the apartheid regime with the opportunity to move the boundary of its conflict with the ANC from the Limpopo to the Zambezi River.

To me this seemed to be a panic measure brought about by the concerns expressed by the OAU. But much more interesting was the information that George gave about the selection of people who would form the first wave of fighters to go into Rhodesia. All seemed to be comrades from Kongwa who were considered by the leadership to be dissidents. A large proportion came from the Natal group and 'Pat', 'Mntungwa', 'Ali' and I were on the list. This, we believed, was an exercise not only to placate the OAU but also to be rid of so-called dissidents.

In the next few days we had many discussions about what our next move should be. What was certain was that we were determined not to be used as cannon-fodder. However, where could we start? 'Ali' insisted we should make our way south, travelling by night and staying under cover during the day until we got to South Africa. I, on the other hand, was determined that, if we left, we should not be caught, no matter where we went.

There was a lot of soul-searching. 'Ali', in particular, was very concerned about abandoning the struggle. He was adamant that we could make our way to South Africa and rejoin the struggle inside the country. I fully understood his reasoning and agreed with him, to a point. But I was not convinced that we would get very far heading south. It took a few more days of serious discussion, as we debated the repercussions if we were to travel north. The question was finally resolved when we received news that a number of comrades who had left Kongwa had been arrested very close to the Zambian border.

This convinced us that all eyes would be focused on the south and that we would easily be identified if we surfaced in a public area en route there. Our descriptions would be circulated to the authorities immediately after it was discovered that we had left and, as a result, we would be picked up. But the decision to head north was not taken lightly, because this meant effectively abandoning the struggle. We wrestled with the idea for some time and changed our minds a number of times, swayed by different arguments. The reaction of our comrades inside and outside South Africa was an important focus and played constantly on our minds before we took the final decision.

Having done so, we were faced with the task of co-ordinating a plan that would include Omar. I had explained to 'Ali' that I would not leave without Omar, and he fully agreed. We had saved up a bit of money, but it was not enough. We could not ask Charlie or anyone close to us because they would be the first people to be questioned. We thought of a number of people who were sympathetic to our plight and identified Dr Parekh. 'Ali' made an excuse to see the doctor for a slight ailment and, since I was responsible for him, I was excused from going to the shop and accompanied him. As we were about to enter the surgery we bumped into 'Pat' and Albert coming out and embraced each other.

Albert walked away, giving us the opportunity to talk. 'Pat' said he was well aware of Joe's plan and that he, 'Pat', was going ahead with it, come what may. Although he acknowledged that the idea of fighting our way through Rhodesia was total madness and an ill-conceived strategy and that the plan smacked of ulterior motives and most of the comrades who went would perish far from the borders of South Africa, he would not back out. He would rather die fighting. But he understood our position and advised us that if we could get away we should do so as soon as possible. He had heard that the plan was to move us out to the front by late July or early August. We shook hands firmly and 'Pat' had tears in his eyes as we parted.

'Ali' and I went in to see Doctor Parekh and explained the situation and our intention. He went out and came back, handing us 400 shillings. We now had just over 600 shillings. 'Ali' contacted a colleague of the trade unionist he had met in prison and we met him outside the camp perimeter. We told him what we planned and said we needed contacts to take us across to Nairobi. He listened carefully and told us to meet him the following day. This we did, and he told us that we should travel to Arusha, where we would be met at the bus terminal by a contact who would brief us on the next stage. We had no choice but to accept this offer, since we had no other options open to us but to trust him and hope for the best.

All this sounded vague, but he convinced us that we should not worry, arrangements would be in hand, but we needed to give dates. So we decided to leave on 26 June. This was South African Freedom Day, the day the ANC commemorated the adoption of the Freedom Charter, and all the officials would be celebrating it. Not much attention would be paid to the fact that we were missing and we could get to Arusha by the next morning. All this time I had managed to keep in touch with Omar, using Latin-based alphabet text in Gujarati, to outline our plans. I now had to get 350 shillings to Omar well before this date, as well as give him details about taking a taxi to meet us at the Arusha bus terminal and bringing Karl with him.

CHAPTER 18

Waiting, planning and getting out

I could not risk sending the money and final instructions to Omar through the ANC transport. But there was another way: I was sure I could trust Mr Harman, and he had an office in Dar. So I told Japan that I had to go and see the clearing agent, Shamshu, about getting clearance for goods from East Germany and, on the way, stopped over at Harman's office. Mr Harman, who was there, said his truck was leaving for Kongwa that evening. I handed him the envelope, with strict instructions to hand it to Omar and to no-one else. He should wait for Omar, who would visit his shop on the weekend. Under no circumstances should he contact the camp.

But I hadn't calculated on Omar sending a reply via Mr Harman and, a week before our planned departure, Mr Harman made a big mistake. He called the ANC office to tell them that there was a letter for me from Omar and could I come to collect it. Whoever was in charge at the office sent Albert to pick me up from the shop and accompany me to Harman's. He was told to check the contents of the letter and, if necessary, bring it to the office. This scared me almost to death and, when I picked up the letter, I told Mr Harman not to call the office again. I opened the envelope at a slight distance from Albert and saw there was a five-shilling note along with a letter. I took out the money and showed it to Albert. He nodded okay and, fortunately, did not ask to check to see if there was anything else in the envelope.

Relieved, I put the envelope in my pocket, slipping out the letter at the same time, just in case Albert had second thoughts. As a result, Albert reported to the office that Omar had sent me some money. Omar's letter acknowledged receipt of the money from me and confirmed that he would make an excuse to go to Dodoma and take a cab from there.

I was concerned that the commanders might not give him permission to leave the camp and, particularly, to go to Dodoma. He should have stuck to going to the village to make his way from there to Dodoma without alerting the camp commander. But there was nothing I could do and it was up to Omar to make the move and meet us. However, I was still deeply concerned. What if he did not make the meeting? We had left South Africa together and if 'Ali' and I were successful in getting away and Omar did not make it, it would be on my conscience for the rest of my life.

That evening I told 'Ali' what had happened and he was furious with Mr Harman and cursed Omar. This was a close shave and I was praying that there would be no more communications from Omar. However, I was pleased that, against all odds and with Omar all that distance away, we had, within a month, managed to create a network to establish a line of communication. This had seemed impossible when we started out. Now we waited and prayed that we would not be moved to Zambia before 26 June.

While we waited we received constant feedback about what was happening in Kongwa and one story that reached us had a comic side to it: it seemed that the ANC had evidence that a comrade, Solomon Bopela, was an apartheid spy. He was convicted and sentenced to death by firing squad. The execution detail comprised a commander and three comrades, all of whom had been provided with rifles.

The firing squad drove with Solomon to a remote area of bush a few miles from Kongwa, where they stood him in position. He stood to attention and the four backed away for some distance, stood in a line, raised their weapons and the commander gave the order: 'Ready, aim, fire!' Shots rang out and Solomon collapsed. The comrades then moved off to an open patch of ground and started digging the grave. But when they had finished and went to retrieve the body, it was nowhere to be found. Having searched the area without success, they returned to camp, where it was assumed they had completed their mission. The firing squad was certainly not going to admit that anything had gone wrong, but the story eventually got out.

The reason it did was that Solomon managed to make it to Zambia and handed himself over to the Zambian authorities in Lusaka. He told how, as the commander had given the order to fire, he had dropped, perhaps as much in fright as anything else. As he lay there, he could not believe that the firing squad had not come over to check on whether or not he was dead. And while the squad was engrossed in digging his grave, he crawled away into the bush before running for his life. The Zambian authorities deported him to South Africa, where he served with the Special Branch, working against the ANC.

As we sat in Dar, waiting and worrying, Joe Modise arrived one evening. He was swankily dressed in new clothes and asked me for a glass of water. I fetched it, but, as I handed it to him, he motioned to me to put the glass to his mouth. I was tempted to spill the lot down his new shirt, but instead complied. He drank the water with his arms dangling by his sides. When he had finished, he asked Japan for a cloth and motioned him to dab his mouth.

This took me back to when he had asked me in Czechoslovakia to polish his boots. This time he was showing that now he could not be disobeyed. I was inwardly fuming when Joe announced that we needed to get ready because we would soon be moving out. I froze, thinking we might be leaving later that day, but Joe said he would be remaining in Dar for a few more days.

I think I visibly relaxed. But we did have a contingency plan in the event that we were to be moved south suddenly. We had arranged with our trade union contact that we would leave the camp immediately and make our way to his house. He had a parcel of clothes to hold for us and this he would bring to us on 26 June. If we had to leave early, he had agreed to keep us undercover until then.

As the day drew closer we decided that we should inform Mosie of our plans. We had had a lot of discussions with him about the incursion that was being planned for Zimbabwe and had told him we thought it was futile and why we thought it was happening. He did not respond one way or the other, so we did not know what he was thinking. However, out of courtesy, we decided we would tell him. Three days to go and there was much talk in the ANC office about a 26 June celebration on the Monday. To me that sounded promising. Most of the officials would get so boozed that by the time they sobered up we would be well away from Dar.

Then, unexpectedly, Charlie returned from his overseas trip two days early. I had hoped that we would be gone before his arrival, scheduled for 27 June, so there would be no question of having to see him on the Monday. I had already made sure that all the financial records were up to date and I had had no access to the till; it was Japan's role to check it, while I recorded the receipts on paper. I had done this so that I could not be accused of theft – if we were caught that would be the most likely charge I would face.

Early on the Sunday night before we were scheduled to leave and, I suppose, formally hand back the shop to Charlie, 'Ali' and I took Mosie aside and told him we were leaving. We gave very little information in case he was questioned. He listened impassively and just remarked that it looked as though Gerald (Lockman), who had previously absconded, was the advance guard and we were following him. That was good and we let him believe that we would head south. However, because Mosie was known to be a friend, we suggested that he leave the camp at least an hour before us to avoid anyone thinking he was in any way connected with our absconding.

In the meantime, 'Ali' and I went over our plan: we would meet our contact at 4.30pm at the bus terminal, because the bus to Arusha was scheduled to leave at 4.45pm, and we did not want to be early in case any ANC operatives spotted us when driving past. The contact had our tickets and the name of another contact who would, we were assured, be waiting for us at the terminal in Arusha. He had been given our descriptions, so we could easily be identified and all arrangements for accommodation had been made. In Arusha we would be given further instructions.

That night we were unable to sleep. I kept thinking about all the things that could go wrong and interfere with our plan. What if Mampuru refused us permission to leave the camp? What if we were spotted by someone from the office before we boarded the bus, or were stopped halfway to our destination? And what would we do if our contact did not turn up or if Omar did not make it? On top of it all, I hoped not to get that awful motion sickness on the bus. And so I waited, just wanting daylight to come so we could be on our way.

We woke up at the usual time and followed our usual routine and, although we were both tense, I don't think we showed it. The first hurdle was to approach Mampuru and request permission for a day out. I told him it would be nice to meet up with Charlie and brief him about the shop and he agreed. I then went to Mosie and told him to move out before us. He left, and we followed about half an hour later, but decided not to board the bus from our usual stop. Instead, we walked three stops further on down the road, sure that Mosie was far ahead of us. But when the bus appeared and we boarded, there was Mosie sitting near the back and pretending not to know us. At least we were on our way and the whole situation suddenly seemed very funny.

Without so much as a backward glance at Mosie, we got off the bus at the beachfront, clutching brown paper carrier bags. It was 12.30pm and we needed to stay out of sight for four hours. The beachfront was not the place to be, so we slipped into a side street, a place where we were unlikely to see any ANC person wandering around or driving through. Time dragged. An hour later we bought some food, found a secluded spot and ate.

There were still hours to go when we strolled past a cinema showing an Indian movie called *Waqt* (Time). This was perfect, since Indian movies last for up to three hours. The film, in Hindi, was billed as a mystery/romance. I don't think either of us remembered much about it and we had to leave before the movie ended, but, in the darkness of the cinema, we no longer had to look over our shoulders all the time.

As it was, we slightly mistimed leaving the cinema and were five minutes late for our scheduled meeting, but our contact was there with our belongings, which we put into our carrier bags. He gave us a broad smile and embraced us, putting me at ease. He told us that our contact in Arusha was named Felix. He would be waiting for us and would recognise us. He then helped us board the bus. We were the first passengers to get on and settled in the middle, hoping that we would not be recognised and also hoping that Omar was on his way.

As darkness descended the bus reached the outskirts of Dar and moved onto a gravel road dotted with potholes that, when the bus hit them, lifted us from our seats. I dozed off at short intervals, with my mind full of the events of the past few days, while also worrying about Omar and what might be waiting ahead. After some time I suddenly became aware that I felt no motion sickness. My stomach was tight, but I had had nothing to eat that evening and, although I was tempted, decided against drinking or eating anything as we drove through the night.

The bus finally came to a stop at the Arusha bus terminal at 10.30am. The terminal was bustling with all sorts of activity and we looked out of the window trying to identify our contact, at the same time hoping that the ANC had not alerted the authorities countrywide to be on the lookout for us. Warily, we got off the bus and saw a number of police mingling with the crowd. As casually as we could, we walked past them and were ignored.

Then, from among the crowd, a young man stepped in front of us and asked: 'Ali'? It was Felix. He shook our hands and led us away. I was looking around frantically for Omar, but there was no sign of him. As we made our way out of the terminal I asked Felix if he had seen anybody arriving by taxi, among them an Indian. He said no and I started panicking, imagining what might be happening to Omar and whether he was back in Kongwa under arrest.

Did one of the comrades he might have approached about leaving give him up? I felt really guilty and even the fact that 'Ali' and I had made it that far did not seem like cause for celebration. But while I worried about Omar, we were also still not in the clear. Felix said it would be best if we moved away from the area. He would take us to his flat and would go back to see if the others had arrived. The two-bedroom flat was about a mile from the terminal and, after giving us some refreshments, he returned to the terminal.

CHAPTER 19

Surprise arrivals on the road to Nairobi

In the half hour or so that Felix was away from the flat 'Ali' and I hardly exchanged a word. We just sat there nervously waiting. But then Felix opened the door, followed by Omar, Socrates and Alfred Shabangu (Pinkie). We grabbed and embraced each other, laughing. All the pressure and tension evaporated. It was some time before I registered my surprise at seeing Socrates and Pinkie, because I was expecting Karl.

We had so much to catch up on. The new arrivals told us their trip from Dodoma had been long and uneventful, except that, at some stopover, a couple of locals tried to attack Omar for no apparent reason. Socrates, who spoke quite fluent Swahili, stepped in and managed to disengage Omar. There were no other incidents and, since none of us was going to leave the safety of the flat, we enjoyed a meal and caught up on the news of Kongwa in the six months since I had left.

It seemed there had been no real change in the situation. Morale, they all agreed, was low, and a big split had opened up between the Eastern and Western Cape groups. Although there was some movement, with comrades leaving the camp, they were mainly from Natal and the feeling among the Cape groups was that they were being left behind. Most of those included in the groups being drafted out were the so-called dissidents, who, at some time or another, had objected to or defied the camp authorities.

This seemed to confirm what George had told us and provided even more justification for our decision to leave. In addition, the three from Kongwa said that there was an increase in the number of people jumping camp and the level of drinking had got even worse. Before we went to sleep, at around midnight, I managed to have a few minutes with Omar on his own and asked him why he had not brought Karl with him. He told me that Karl was on the list to leave camp and head south. He was confident that the army was finally going back home and had declined the offer to abscond. Perhaps, I thought at the time, he, like 'Pat', felt it was better to die fighting trying to get home.

In the process of our discussions that night we discovered that the flat we were in belonged to a chap called Thabo, a South African. He and another comrade, Professor, had been the first people to try and leave the ANC and MK when they were in Morogoro. They were caught, returned to the ANC, and were placed in an isolation cell, where they were maltreated by the Morogoro camp commander, Ranka, and a comrade named Troy. They were told that they would remain under lock and key until the liberation of South Africa. However, with the help of a number of Tanzanians, they had managed to escape and head to northern Tanzania.

We discovered these details when Thabo, a practising lawyer working in Arusha, arrived. He told us about the treatment he had received when he was arrested and he hoped that, one day, he would get the opportunity to meet up with Ranka and Troy to take his revenge. Thabo left us before midnight, saying we should relax, all the arrangements had been made on both sides of the border. He wished us well and that was the last we saw of him.

In the morning we discussed with Felix the options open to us in crossing the border. It was obvious that if we took the regular bus service we were likely to be stopped and asked to produce travel documents. Socrates and Pinkie could manage to travel in this way because they could speak Swahili and could pass as locals. Felix decided that they should go ahead and meet us in Nairobi. 'Ali', Omar and I would take another route, leave the bus at the nearest town to the border and cross by foot. Felix said he had to go out to meet a contact to confirm our travel arrangements to the border. After he left we realised that he had not parted with any details about what arrangements had been made for us to cross the border.

There was nothing we could do and Felix returned with snacks that afternoon and told us that we three were leaving the next morning at 10am by bus to a small village, Kibouni, near the border and at the foot of Mt Kilimanjaro. There we would be met by a contact who had arranged a sleepover. We would cross the border the following morning. We were all disappointed to be spending another night in Tanzania and worried that the longer we stayed, the more chance there was of us being arrested. However, we were at the mercy of others and we had to go along with the arrangements.

Confined to the flat, I wondered what action the ANC had taken to track us down. They would, of course, have informed the Tanzanian authorities about our departure and the Tanzanian army and police would be on the lookout. I also thought about what Charlie must be thinking. He would almost certainly have rushed to the shop to check if there was any money missing from the till. Although I had taken every precaution to show that I could not have taken anything, I remained concerned that I would be accused of theft. But I also relaxed slightly, imagining that all the resources used looking for us would be concentrated on the route south.

In the midst of my musings, I overheard a conversation between 'Ali' and Socrates about the people who had left the camp in the past few weeks. Socrates told of the visit a month earlier of Joe Modise and OR Tambo. OR addressed the comrades, assuring them that arrangements had been made to move all the people out of the camp to Zambia and that the movement in South Africa was preparing to receive the soldiers of Umkhonto. Joe followed this speech by calling on everyone to be battle-ready. He said that in the next few weeks the focus should be on physical fitness for the journey to South Africa. Within two months, the camp at Kongwa would be empty and comrades would be given a final briefing in Zambia before leaving for home.

I asked Socrates if there was any indication that the way to South Africa that they proposed would be through joint operations with ZAPU and that comrades would have to fight their way through Rhodesia. But he was sure that neither Tambo nor Joe had made any mention of joint operations. The impression left was that the move was directly to South Africa, because a lot of emphasis was on the readiness of the internal movement to receive the combatants. This had given a huge boost to morale and was the reason that Karl had decided not to join us. 'Ali' asked if anyone had questioned Tambo and Joe about how it would be possible to move hundreds of people so quickly across borders and into South Africa without the apartheid government knowing about it. In any case, did the logistical capacity exist to carry out such a move?

Socrates admitted that there had been no questions. Comrades were too excited. It seemed that at last they were going home and that was all that mattered. After Joe and OR left, the comrades were almost all up early jogging and performing physical exercises throughout the day, preparing for their return home. Only a small number did not join this regime, most of them owing to medical conditions. There were also a few cynics, but what surprised 'Ali' and me was that Omar, Socrates and Pinkie admitted to actually believing Modise and Tambo. It was only as the weeks went by and nothing much happened that some doubt set in. 'Ali' explained to them then that the two leaders had deliberately misled the comrades by withholding the information that what was planned was a joint operation with ZAPU in Rhodesia, the strategy being to first liberate Rhodesia and then move on to South Africa.

The discussion was interrupted when Felix entered to brief us on our journey the next day, and we were given our bus tickets. Socrates's and Pinkie's tickets were to Nairobi, where they would make their way to a particular hotel. On our bus, Omar and I would occupy seats apart from one another. Felix and 'Ali' would sit together as travelling companions. This would ensure that we were not seen as a group and would not raise any suspicions. We all retired early and, surprisingly, I managed to fall asleep straight away. Omar was up early and we all had tea and buttered bread and jam before exiting the flat at short intervals, following Felix and 'Ali', who strode ahead with Omar and me behind them and Socrates and Pinkie some distance behind us.

When we reached the bus terminal, Socrates and Pinkie made their way to the Nairobi bus while we followed Felix, heading nervously toward our bus, keeping an eye out for any police. Our nerves were playing tricks on us and we were surprised that we attracted no attention because we were both convinced that we looked conspicuous. Obviously we did not, and the people around us went on with their usual business. There were only two policemen in sight and they were deep in conversation with a woman at the other end of the terminal. Nonetheless, as we settled into our seats as instructed, we were still anxious, willing the bus to move off.

Finally the engine started and we were on our way out of Arusha. I had now become a practised traveller and no longer suffered the miseries of motion sickness. About time, I supposed, having travelled so much. As a result, I could quite enjoy the journey, as we stopped at a number of small villages and towns. At some of these, Felix would provide us with refreshments. At one point I asked 'Ali' if he had given any money to Felix because he was providing all the food. He hadn't, he said. This had been taken care of by the trade union contact in Dar.

It was a long trip and we reached our destination, a small village, as the sun was setting. When the bus stopped we stepped out and gathered as a group as a Land Rover pulled up. Felix spoke to the driver and signalled to us to climb aboard. We jumped in and 30 minutes later reached a building where we were led into a room with chairs and sofas. We learned that this was an Outward Bound Centre. This meant nothing to us and we were ignorant of its purpose, but as we stood there, a man walked in and greeted Felix. We realised from his accent that he was English and he took Felix aside and had a long chat with him. We were unable to hear the conversation, but, from the reaction of the man, it was obvious he was not too happy having us at the centre.

Eventually, however, we were escorted to a dining area and provided with meals and drinks. Over the table 'Ali' asked what the problem was and Felix said, because we were South Africans, the director of the centre was worried that he would get into trouble with the Tanzanian authorities for assisting us. As a result, he, Felix, had to make sure that we were out of the centre as early as possible the next morning.

We were given beds for the night and breakfast the following morning. Not knowing anything about the Outward Bound Trust, we assumed that the centre was run by the American Peace Corps and were extremely wary. There had, for example, been US Peace Corps settlements very close to the camps in Kongwa and right on the doorstep of the training camps of other African liberation movements. It seemed to us highly likely that these were fronts for the CIA, although we had no evidence. We had similar suspicions about the Outward Bound Centre and were keen to leave, getting up early in the morning.

The same Land Rover that had picked us up in Arusha took us across the Kenyan border at a remote crossing point and dropped us off in the small town of Loitokitok. From this point, we were told, we should take the bus to Nairobi. But after the Land Rover had left, we discovered that the next bus would only leave in several days. We could not hang around in the town for fear of attracting attention. Felix checked and said that we needed to make our way, if need be, on foot, to Emali, which was about 105km away. There we would meet regular transport from Mombasa to Nairobi. Busses to Nairobi apparently arrived in Emali at 6pm every evening. Having spent fruitless hours looking for taxis or friendly drivers who might be going our way, we finally decided to walk to Emali.

One problem immediately presented itself: we had no maps. But Felix, sounding optimistic, assured us that he had travelled the road before and we would be able to make it. So we bought food and drinks and made our way along the road to Emali. The terrain was flat and walking was easy, so initially we covered a good deal of ground fast. But after about two hours we slowed down to a less brisk pace. Along the way we met a number of Masai men carrying spears, who looked at us in amazement.

Every so often we checked with Felix and he assured us we were on the right track. Another couple of hours later, and with our pace slowing even more, we noticed a vehicle coming up behind us. It was the Land Rover from the centre, with the same driver who had dropped us in the village we had left that morning. He had obviously been able to use the vehicle again and had decided to help us out. He also informed us that we were walking through what he referred to as a 'restricted area', a wildlife park. We should get aboard because there were lions and other dangerous animals around.

As we drove our imaginations ran wild and we began to imagine the outlines of lions and other beasts in the shadows of trees and in the distance. We expressed our shock to Felix, who replied casually that, in all his trips, he had never seen any wildlife. This was less than convincing and we were sure that, like us, this was the first such trip he had undertaken. Above all, we were grateful we were in the Land Rover.

We got to the bus station in Emali 30 minutes before the bus to Nairobi arrived. Among the people at the stop preparing to board were a number of people of Asian origin. This was welcome because Omar, 'Ali' and I no longer looked conspicuous and could relax. We had successfully crossed into Kenya, and no longer looked like obvious interlopers as we headed for Nairobi. My travel sickness and our nervousness had evaporated and, after a number of stops along the way, the bus finally arrived in the Kenyan capital at 10pm.

CHAPTER 20

Name changes and refugee status

With Felix leading the way we walked for about an hour before we reached a hotel. Felix entered and went straight to a room and knocked. Omar and I followed behind 'Ali'. The door opened and there were Pinkie and Socrates. With them was an African American who, we were told, was a resident of the hotel and lived in the room. We were all relieved to see one another and, as we sat down, some snacks were passed around. It soon became obvious that this was the only room available to us; that all seven of us would have to make ourselves as comfortable as possible. Nobody mentioned what might happen should the hotel staff come by to check on this now overcrowded room.

The next morning we were up early and out of the room and hotel, without breakfast. Felix led the way to the United Nations High Commissioner for Refugees (UNHCR) to enable us to register as refugees. He told us that once we were registered, the ANC had no jurisdiction and could not return us to Tanzania, but we were not so sure about that. It was a long trek to the offices, which were at the far end of Nairobi. Going through the centre of this bustling city was an eye-opener for we who had spent years in isolated rural camps or the relatively humdrum life of Dar. It certainly was a far cry from what we had become used to.

On reaching the UNHCR we approached the reception desk and informed a young Kenyan man that we were from South Africa and had come to register as refugees. His comment took us by complete surprise: 'Comrades, you are in Africa and therefore, do not consider yourselves as refugees. You are Africans.' What a welcome!

We were interviewed in a group, given forms to complete, and it was at this point that I changed my name from Aminoddin Kajee to Amin Cajee, with the intention and hope of misleading anyone who sought to track us down in the future and perhaps return us to Tanzania. The others also changed their names. We were all fearful of what might happen to us if we were returned to be tried as deserters by the ANC. 'Ali' became Hussain Jacobs, Omar Moosa changed to Omar Bhamjee, Socrates to Maurice Mothombeni (he later reverted to his original name, Abe Moloi) and Pinkie to Alfred Shabangu. The names were accepted and we were taken across the road to the offices of the Kenyan Christian Council to formally register as refugees.

The lay preacher who was in charge was surprised and impressed to see Indians in Africa registering as refugees and immediately bonded with our group. He told us that we would each receive a weekly stipend of 50 shillings, to be collected every Monday, and we managed to convince him to give us an extra, 'one-off' allowance because we had very little clothing.

It was at this time that we met a number of other South Africans, all former members of the PAC. We were the very first ANC arrivals. They warmed to Socrates and Pinkie, but kept their distance from the three of us. The fact that we were of Indian extraction was still a problem for them. We were taken to Eastleigh, a suburb of Nairobi, where most of the exiles lived and Alfred (Pinkie) and Maurice (Socrates) were offered accommodation in a PAC residence. The offer was not extended to us, but I told them to take what was offered; we would find our own way round and we would stay in contact through the Kenyan Christian Council.

Omar, Hussain ('Ali') and I decided our best bet was to find a mosque and see if we could find accommodation there. We asked around and were directed to a mosque in Eastleigh where we waited for the late afternoon prayer and approached the imam. He said that they had a *musafir khana* (accommodation for travellers) but that this was limited to three nights' accommodation. This suited us well since it gave us time to seek an alternative arrangement. And we had some money to see us through until our next stipend.

We moved into the *musafir khana* and, early the next day, we took time to find our bearings and to check the roads and busses into the city. Eastleigh was a predominantly African area, where we were stared at by the locals and felt uncomfortable. A degree of segregation still applied here and we decided to seek accommodation in an Asian area, where we would blend in better. We spent that first day scouting an Asian area close to Eastleigh without any luck. The next day we went to the Central Mosque to make contacts but were disappointed by the reception. As Muslims we had expected to be received sympathetically, provided with information and put in touch with a welfare organisation that would provide us with assistance in the short term. We were ignored and told that they could offer us no help.

It was late that afternoon, while we were walking in another part of the city, that we noticed an Indian vegetarian restaurant that advertised: 'Eat as much as you can – meals for a shilling.' We had not had a decent meal for some time – it had been tea and fat cakes for most of the way, so we decided to make an investment and eat for the whole week. By the time the third helping reached our table we were full. It was then that a young chap who had been watching us closely came up to have a chat.

The young man introduced himself as Banu. He was curious about us as we had obviously been very hungry. So we explained ourselves and our circumstances. He listened carefully and when we had finished said he had a room we could use. There were no beds, but he would provide us with mats and blankets. We could not believe our luck and arranged to meet him the next day at the same place at 5pm.

Banu lived in a three-bedroom flat on the second floor of a building within the city area with his wife, whom we referred to as Bhabi (sister-in-law). She did not speak a word of English, but thankfully Omar was able to open the lines of communication in Gujarati. The couple were Hindus and he worked at the Bank of Baroda. They not only provided us with accommodation and food, they refused payment. They would also take us along when they visited friends and we became acquainted with Sailesh, who also worked at the Bank of Baroda, and his wife, and with Prakash, who worked for a coffee bean company, and his wife and young son, Dermesh. We called all the wives Bhabi, and we would pop in to have meals and make ourselves at home.

We simply could not go on in this way, however, and it was well into three weeks when we decided that we had overstayed this wonderful welcome and hospitality. We spoke to Prakash, who lived in the Ngara area, and he directed us to a building close to him where an Ismaili family ran a boarding house. That is where we landed next – sharing a room, with breakfast, lunch and evening meals.

Through the UNHCR we got scholarships to study and I enrolled at Ravel's School to complete O levels in English and British constitutional law. The others also enrolled and gained O levels while Omar continued to study accountancy at a private school. I found employment with a Mr Amin at the Atlantic Travel Service for a short period, doing accounts. In the meantime, Hussain made contact with the owner of a restaurant, the Flora, and, through this contact, was able to secure a four-bedroom house in the suburb of Pangani.

By that time we had met up with another South African refugee, called Sidiqi, a painter and former member of the PAC who was married and had a two-year-old daughter. He shared the accommodation and costs with us. The next-door neighbour was initially unimpressed by our arrival.

Perhaps rightly so because he was married with three children and was also responsible for the welfare of his mother and four unmarried sisters. The arrival of three bachelors on his doorstep must have seemed a major threat. However, we behaved ourselves well and, within a short period, and thanks to the fact that we were also Muslim, we became very close to the family and were well received.

Through an Ismaili contact introduced to us by 'Hussain' I managed to land a job in the accounts department of a local trading company, GS Martin. Sidiqi and his family left the accommodation and 'Maurice', 'Alfred' and Pepes, a former PAC member, joined us in the house. We also made contact with a number of other South Africans. 'Hussain', who was from Pretoria, established links with members of the Ismaili community who were originally from that city.

Among our new acquaintances was a teacher, Solly, who taught at a private English language school, and another, Fakir Salie, whom I recognised from Vrededorp. He had been an active member of the ANC and possibly MK. Two former Pretoria residents were Goolam Hajee and his wife, who came from an Afrikaner background. The couple had fled South Africa to avoid being charged under the Immorality Act. They regularly invited us over for a meal.

We also made friends with an Indian woman who was married to an English expatriate, and through her we met a Swedish film director, Vilgot Shurman. He was very keen to hear about our experiences and gave us his contact address if we ever came to Sweden, a destination we thought seriously about as we were planning to make our way to Europe. As a possible insurance policy should anything happen to us, we also provided Vilgot with a written outline of roughly what we had been through and our analysis of the situation, something Vilgot kept.

Walking around Nairobi one day Omar and I bumped into a young couple from Belgium, Karl and Lyddy Hoogenhout, who were travelling through Africa and had, at some point, been in South Africa. They were looking for accommodation and, since we had been in a similar situation not too long ago, we invited them to stay with us. Karl had with him what we thought was a monkey (it was a bushbaby, or galago) that they were taking to Belgium. We became good friends with the couple and they stayed with us for a month. On leaving they said we would be welcome to stay with them if we ever got to Belgium. We thanked them, but were sure that we would never have cause to do so. It seemed the most unlikely destination, yet, as it turned out, it was to play a major role in our lives.

Dearest Brother Amin,
Today on your departure
from us, I feel we should
have never met, because
I cant bear the pain
of you leaving us.

You will be ever reme-
mbered by me as a
true and sincere
comrade, one day
inshallah we shall mee
in much happier moment
then this.

From
Baboo (Bobby)

The other Amin Cajee ('Bobby') the a-political recruit who accompanied his friend Abdul Satar Tayob ('Stanley') to Czechoslovakia. Both turned themselves in to the police on their return to South Africa.

At the time there were many discussions among the South Africans we had met about the goings on 'back home'. On one of these occasions Salie Fakir mentioned that before he had left South Africa he had come across a brief article in a newspaper that mentioned two men who had recently arrived in the country from India. They had given themselves up to the Special Branch and the report, he told us, had said that they had provided the police with a wealth of information about their training in Czechoslovakia. We were shocked. It was obvious that the article referred to 'Stanley' and 'Bobby'. If they had handed over any group photographs these probably included Omar and me as well as 'Ali' and Zee.

To our horror 'Ali' and I recalled that at one of our last meetings in Kongwa with Joe Modise he had made specific reference to 'Bobby' and 'Stanley', saying they had managed to enter South Africa undetected and were operating underground; that they had been told to expect us and would be our contacts when we reached South Africa. This meant that the ANC had no idea that they had given themselves up immediately after they disembarked from the ship in Durban. Or perhaps there was something more sinister afoot?

✳ ✳ ✳

More than 40 years later I received a telephone call from 'the other Amin Cajee' – 'Bobby' – who was in South Africa. He said he wanted to apologise for what he and 'Stanley' had done. They had been very frightened when they arrived back in Durban and had decided to tell the police everything and get on with their lives.

'So we just handed over everything,' he said. This also meant, presumably, the informal photographs taken of all of us in Czechoslovakia and perhaps any manuals or communications equipment they may have had with them. All in all it could not have added much to anything the police already knew, certainly about Omar and me. They had probably had information about us from as early as our arrival in Dar es Salaam and definitely from our detention in London. 'Bobby' also told me his son had died in a motorcycle accident and he insisted he had not intended any of us to come to harm. I felt sorry for him and did not press him about what other price he had paid, if any.

In early 2015, while working on this book and thinking so much about the past, I decided during a visit to South Africa to track down Bobby' and 'Stanley'. I heard that Amin Cajee, who I assumed was 'Bobby', had died in a car accident. I was able to track 'Stanley' down to a shop he owns in Vereeniging, south of Johannesburg. It had been 50 years since we parted in Czechoslovakia and we did not recognise each other, both grey bearded and with an absence of hair on our heads.

Five minutes into this encounter, and after I introduced myself and addressed him as 'Stanley', he went into a mode of complete denial, did not remember me, had no recollection of meeting me. I studied him for a while and then asked about 'Bobby', who, I said, had died in a car accident. He immediately corrected me. 'No,' he said, 'that was another Amin Cajee. "Bobby" died of a heart attack.' He was jolted by this slip-up. But having admitted that he knew 'Bobby', he only complained that he had not received a veteran's pension while, he said, 'Bobby' had got one.

He wanted to know if there was anything I could do to help with his pension application, went to a filing cabinet, pulled out a file and handed it to me. I flipped through the file and saw testimonials from Mosie Moola, Ahmed Kathrada, James April (George Driver) and others supporting his application. So I asked him about George and he responded immediately that he had seen him at the Planet Hall in Fordsburg one Saturday night just before he was arrested.

As I made my way out of the shop he kept saying he did not remember me.

He followed and asked for the phone number where I was staying, which he noted. Within an hour of my return to Johannesburg he was on the phone and invited me to come down for a braai (barbeque) at his home. I had a very tight schedule and was unable to make it, and there the contact ended.

＊ ＊ ＊

From newer arrivals in Nairobi we heard that when word got around in Kongwa that we had succeeded in evading the long arm of the ANC, individual comrades and groups decided to follow suit. We were acquainted with one of these new arrivals, Oompie. He informed us that Joe Modise had been the reason for their decision to come north. He had been scathing about our departure and had promised that even if we were in Kenya the ANC would pursue us and we would soon be brought back to face the consequences of our actions.

This information, and the fact that we had not been brought back, made them realise that travelling to Kenya instead of going south was a better bet for freedom. But they gave us some bad news about the Harman family. They had been taken into custody by the Tanzanian authorities, questioned and accused of helping us escape. Although they had had nothing to do with it, their business was closed down and they lost everything. We felt very guilty because they had had no idea of our plans, but I had used their drivers on two occasions to get letters to Omar.

Oompie also told us about the briefings they had received in Kongwa. It had been announced that they would be going through Rhodesia to make their way to South Africa, but there was no mention that they would be engaged in any combat. The only reference Joe Modise apparently made was that if they met opposition from the Rhodesian forces, ZAPU would be in control and would lead them out. However, they should be prepared to fight. A lot of emphasis was placed on the fact that their route had been worked out and that South Africa was their destination.

CHAPTER 21

Zimbabwe, Wankie and looking to Europe

According to Oompie, before he left there was disquiet among the majority of the comrades in Kongwa and this led to a number of people leaving the camp. To stop this exodus the leaders decided to move people out to Zambia. We were still digesting this information when there was a surprise arrival in Nairobi – 'Van' (the driver) and his partner, Doreen. 'Van', using his proper name, Vincent Mkhubu, was regarded by the leaders as a loyal comrade and we could not understand why he had travelled to Nairobi. Doreen, on the other hand, was a close friend who came from Natal and was closely linked to Rubin, Karl and the Natal group.

My first response was that 'Van' had been sent as a plant and we were very cautious. Was Doreen being used as his cover? We questioned him closely and, after some time, we became convinced that he was genuine. At one of our earlier meetings 'Van' said that some weeks after we had left the camp he took JB Marks from Morogoro to Dar. JB asked him if he had known us and 'Van' said he had known us well and that he knew my brother Joe in Lusaka. JB remarked that since we were the first to have escaped successfully it was a pity that the skills we employed to carry out our operation had not been used for the benefit of the movement.

We asked 'Van' if he had been to the front and he said he had transported the first group of comrades. These included most of the Natal group. At the point where they were to cross the Zambezi River there was a big flare-up between Joe Modise and 'Pat'. 'Pat' was not happy with the number of ammunition magazines and grenades that had been provided and Joe accused him of being a coward and making excuses for not wanting to go across. 'Pat' challenged Joe to cross with him and not stay in safety on the Zambian side. Joe walked away.

There had also been resistance from a number of comrades who did not want to get into the boats. One of the biggest fears was falling into the crocodile-infested river, because many were unable to swim. 'Van' claimed that a number of boats had capsized while crossing because of the inexperience of the rowers and because some comrades had panicked.

We asked about the ZAPU comrades who were supposed to accompany our chaps. They, we had heard, had experience in crossing the river. 'Van' said that there were a few present, but they stayed mainly in the background and did not interfere. They let Joe, with some others, take charge of the river crossing. It looked, he said, as if the priority was to get as many people as possible across at whatever cost. I asked if Zee was in this group and he said that Zee had been part of a much smaller communications group that had earlier crossed over at the same point to set up a base.

What puzzled me was that if Zee and his group had been ambushed by Rhodesian forces, why were more comrades being sent across at the same point? Surely the Rhodesians would lie in waiting. 'Van' said he had made two trips to the front and had decided that the operation smacked of a suicide mission. Reports were filtering through that we were suffering huge casualties and clashes were reported soon after people had crossed over, confirming that the Rhodesian forces were prepared. It was at this point that he and Doreen had decided to leave.

I thought back to our training days and how the fundamental rules of guerrilla warfare had been ignored. These rules stated that before engaging the enemy, small groups should infiltrate, select terrain and ensure that it is conducive for guerrilla warfare, get to know the terrain, prepare escape routes, know the local language and establish contacts and win over the locals, set up bases and caches of arms and ammunition, establish an intelligence network and gather information on the enemy before increasing the area of operation. I presumed that ZAPU might have had the basic criteria in place for its armed struggle, but how did we fit into the framework with our excursion?

My main concern was that no records appeared to have been kept of comrades who were sent on the mission, so there seemed little likelihood that there would be information about those who gave their lives. Yet their families would need to be notified of the sacrifices made on a badly thought-out military mission. As I was to discover in 1970 when I met my brother Joe in Amsterdam, the situation was even more chaotic at the time of these now much-hailed excursions. Joe had met Joe Modise in Lusaka on several occasions, during which Modise had mentioned to him that I would soon be in Lusaka to be taken to the front line.

He was very concerned for my safety and was not impressed at what he saw around him. What troubled him at the time was that Lusaka seemed to be a hub for South African intelligence, with well-known operatives travelling freely in and out. There was, he felt, a total absence of counter-intelligence operations on behalf of the ANC. Of particular concern was the fact that the impending operations were openly discussed in pubs frequented by both ANC personnel and others.

The most damaging incident he reported was a televised media briefing on the news channel of Zambian television about MK units crossing over from Zambia into Rhodesia. I was shaken by this revelation, thinking it was simply a gross blunder, but, on later reflection, I realised that something public had to be said to placate the OAU, which had been critical of the ANC's complacency. Coverage of a military mission would help. What this showed me was the absence of military input into major decisions that put the lives of many comrades at risk.

Some of those who crossed over on that ill-fated mission, which was later to be hailed by the ANC leadership as the battle of Wankie, managed to evade the Rhodesian patrols and made it into South Africa. Rubin, Karl and Derek were among them. A later group from the Cape, including Chris Hani, faced similar difficulties and several of them, Chris among them, made it across the Botswana border. We also heard that 'Paul Peterson' had become separated from this group as they were evading the Rhodesian and South African forces. He hijacked a car and was tracked down, ambushed, and killed.

As fragments of news filtered our way, we heard that there had also been another joint incursion – this one with Frelimo fighters on the Tanzania/ Mozambique border. The only MK person to have returned safely was called Jele. Neither then nor subsequently did I hear any more about this event. It all seemed so tragic and worrying and we remained concerned that the ANC leadership would try to get us back to make an example of us. We had reached a point where we felt we had get out of Africa. Our target was what we saw as the safety of Europe.

Through a contact we made in the UNHCR we were provided with a letter entitling us to be issued with refugee travel documents and this set the stage for our exit from Kenya. Britain would be our destination because of the common language, the presence of exiles from 'back home' and Omar, and my familiarity with London. However, the UK's strict immigration policies would be a massive hurdle since we did not have passports.

While we planned and studied in Nairobi four very personal events took place. The first was in February 1968, when I was fortunate to meet up with my eldest sister, Quraisha, who was passing through on her way back from Mecca. Since arriving in Nairobi we had established contact with our families and this was the first time I had met any member of the family since I left home in 1962.

Quraisha and I met for an hour during an aircraft refuelling stopover at Nairobi airport. Mr Khan, who had many contacts, managed to get me into the transit lounge at the airport. It was a very emotional time for me and in an hour we managed to exchange information about what had happened to me and to the family.

Later that year Omar's sister, Hajira, passed through Nairobi. She had a visa and stayed with us for a few days and it was another emotional meeting. She also brought news and gifts from my family. A very close family friend of Hussain ('Ali') also passed through, spent several days with us and was able to give Hussain information about his mother.

Then, in early 1969, I heard from my family that my father had been given permission to visit his wife and family in South Africa for the first time in 23 years. He was to join my mother for a pilgrimage to Mecca and they would fly via Nairobi in March of that year. Once again there was only a refuelling stop, but this time the passengers were not allowed to disembark and were kept on the plane.

I was quite frantic, but Mr Khan, who had accompanied me to the airport, managed to get me access to the plane. I was apprehensive about meeting my father since I barely remembered him, having been just four years old when he left on what was supposed to be a visit. But I was excited about seeing my mother again as I walked across to the parked plane and mounted the stairs.

My father must have been warned that I would be coming because as I got near the top of the stairs an elderly man stepped into the doorway and asked: 'Are you Amin?' My throat was constricted, tears welled in my eyes and I think I mumbled, 'Yes.' I was trembling as he held out his arms and said: 'I am your father.' As I recall, these were the only words we exchanged. It was very emotional and he held me tight for a few minutes before he led me into the plane and I saw my mother. We hugged and there were tears in both our eyes.

I don't remember anything more being said and, after a few minutes, I was asked to leave the plane. There was just time to embrace my mother once more and tearfully hug my father. As I left, my mother handed me a paper bag containing some clothes I had left behind in 1962. I left the plane and walked back to the terminal building with mixed feelings of sadness and happiness.

A short while later I heard from my family in South Africa that my father had died in Mecca after performing his pilgrimage. Shortly afterwards my mother returned on her own, again via Nairobi, where, this time, the plane was delayed on the ground for five hours. The passengers were allowed into the transit lounge where Mr Khan and his family provided food and I again met my mother.

It was very emotional, and I was upset to hear that the family had been harassed by the police after Joe had fled. On one of their late night raids the police had implied that both Joe and I were in custody, but did not say where. My mother was terrified that we might have returned to the country, where torture and deaths in detention were well known. She lived with this stress for nearly two years until she heard that I was in Nairobi and Joe in Lusaka.

Other families were in much the same position and Maurice (Socrates) had asked me to give a letter to my mother addressed to his mother. My mother agreed, the two mothers met and the letter was passed on. As a result, Maurice was able to link up again with his family.

Omar and I were very fortunate to have had these early meetings with members of our families, but the meetings were tinged with sadness. Such opportunities did not arise for Hussain ('Ali') and for most of the African comrades, many of whom were never reunited with their families.

CHAPTER 22

A roundabout route to Europe

Some time in 1968 or 1969 Hussain met and began courting a young Scottish expat teacher, Myra. They married and Hussain moved out of our shared house. But we continued meeting and by pooling our resources we raised enough money for four tickets to the UK. Hussain felt that I should be the first to leave, with Myra, to test for any possible difficulties. I should also have an open onward ticket to Brussels that would indicate that I was merely passing through. Once in the UK, with contacts Omar and I had made during our stay there, I would apply for political asylum.

To bolster my onward journey story we wrote to Karl and Lyddy, the couple from Belgium who had stayed with us, and said we intended to visit. In return, they sent us addresses and phone numbers in Antwerp, where they lived, and in Mechelen, where their parents lived. They also gave us a contact at the Belgian embassy in Nairobi, where I managed to secure a visa. Our Plan B was that if I was refused entry into the UK, I should go to Belgium, let the others know and they would have to change plans. In the meantime, it was decided that Hussain would be next to leave, once Myra had set up the process to gain him entry. Omar and Maurice would follow.

Our group managed to put together about £120 in cash that I could provide as proof to the immigration officials that I was not destitute. It would also act as an emergency fund. So, on 1 April 1969 Myra and I flew from Nairobi, bound for London. As usual, throughout the journey I was unable to relax and enjoy the flight. Uncertainty haunted me because of my bad experiences in the past with UK immigration. Myra had given me her parents' address in Yorkshire as a contact point if I had problems getting into the UK.

In the early hours of a grey and wet morning we landed at London's Gatwick airport and proceeded to the immigration counters. Myra went through. I had told her that if I did not follow she should head out, because I would be detained and there was nothing she would be able to do to help me. I walked up to the immigration officer and handed over my UNHCR refugee travel document. He looked at me, examined the pages and asked me to take a seat in the row of chairs set aside for people who were not allowed to go through. It was as I had feared and, I suppose, expected.

After about an hour another officer took me into an interview room and questioned me about the purpose of my visit. I said I wanted a few days in London with friends, handed him Myra's name and address, and said I would later be making my way to Belgium to visit other friends. Judging by the body language and attitude of the officer my story was not believed. He took me to the baggage area and found and searched my bag, obviously hoping to find documents that would contradict my story. There were none. We returned to the interview room and three hours later I was denied entry into the UK.

I said I would like to catch the next flight to Brussels. But the officers said they had decided that I should be put on a flight back to Nairobi. I argued, pointing out that I not only had an open ticket to Brussels, I also had a visa for Belgium. There was some discussion among the officers before they agreed to transfer me to Heathrow for a flight to Brussels.

The officials booked my flight, ordered a taxi and handed my documents and ticket to a Securicor officer who was to escort me to Heathrow and ensure I boarded the plane. I felt like a criminal as I was escorted onto a Sabena flight, and my documents were handed to the airways staff by the security guard. Staff throughout the flight stared and did not try to speak to me, but did provide refreshments, which were appreciated because I had had nothing to eat since a very early breakfast on the flight from Nairobi.

I was very apprehensive when the plane landed at Brussels airport in midafternoon. A stewardess from the flight, clutching my documents, motioned that I should follow her. Together we walked to the immigration desk, where she stepped forward and spoke to the officer. He paged through my travel document and, to my complete surprise, stamped it and motioned me to the exit door to collect my bags. I was in Belgium and free to go where I wanted to.

The full impact of what had happened only hit me later, but I went to the airport information desk and enquired about trains to Brussels and on to Antwerp. After changing some money I found a telephone and called the Antwerp number we had been given: no answer. I waited awhile and tried again. Again no answer. I started to worry as I dialled the Mechelen number. A woman answered in Flemish, which is similar to Afrikaans. I asked for Karl or Lyddy and Karl came to the phone. He was surprised, he said, because they were not expecting any of us so soon, but I was most welcome. He gave me instructions on how to get to Mechelen by train and told me to call from the station.

I arrived in Mechelen that evening. Karl and Lyddy were waiting and we drove to the home of Lyddy's parents, Mr and Mrs Bechart, a lovely couple in their 50s who made me feel at home and offered me tea and cheese sandwiches because Karl had informed them of my dietary restrictions. I was taken to a room on the first floor to leave my bags and freshen up. I would be spending a night here and would go with Karl and Lyddy to Antwerp the next day. So, on this happy and welcoming note, began my stay in Europe.

The Becharts were very grateful for the help we had given their daughter and son-in-law in Nairobi and they and their son, Carl ('With a C to make me different from Karl'), said I could stay as long as I liked. Their generosity was incredible and I felt relaxed, although I worried about getting news to Omar, Maurice and Hussain. This I was able to do after getting back to Antwerp after a fascinating tour of Mechelen, where I was introduced to many of the friends of both Lyddy and Karl and of their parents.

Lyddy and Karl had a one-bedroom apartment and a camp bed was set up for me in their lounge. Lyddy worked and was away early each day while Karl was often around, busy with work for his master's degree. In the first few days I sent off letters to the address that Myra had given me to make contact with Hussain and the others. At the same time, concerned that I should have some alternative destination in case I was again refused entry to the UK, I sent off a letter to the Swedish film director Vilgot Shurman, whom we had met in Nairobi. As I waited for replies I got to know much of Antwerp, either on my own or with Karl as a guide. At the weekends he, Lyddy and I would go to Mechelen to spend time with her parents.

After two weeks in Antwerp I received a reply from Hussain. He had been allowed into the UK and, he wrote, Omar and Maurice were scheduled to follow in the next few weeks. I also received a letter from Vilgot, who wanted me to tape-record our experiences and forward the tape to him. Karl gave me a tape recorder, and over the next few weeks I felt strange hearing myself talking as I spoke into the microphone with difficulty, looking for the delete button and chopping and changing, but I managed to complete the recording and sent it off to Vilgot.

Then a second letter arrived from Hussain. He sent me some money and informed me that he and Myra had an assurance from James Callaghan, the Labour Party Home Secretary, that should I make my way back to London and seek political asylum it would be granted. I was guaranteed entry into the UK. This was rather sudden and the thought of another bad experience and further humiliation made me decide initially not to go. But after a week

I relented, sent my flight details to Hussain and, almost reluctantly, made my way to the airport to board a flight to London. All the past horrors gripped me as the plane landed at Heathrow and I slowly made my way to the immigration desk and presented myself to the officer. I declared that I was applying for political asylum and was told to take a seat.

After a couple of hours I was taken to an interview room and questioned by an officer for at least an hour on the grounds on which I was seeking asylum. I explained my circumstances and my fear of being sent back to Tanzania and handed over to the ANC. At the end of the interview the immigration officer said that I had already been refused entry to the country but would be put into detention until the immigration department heard from the Home Office. I felt quite sick as I was again escorted by a Securicor officer to the baggage area, where I picked up my bag. The officer then took me to what he described as the Queens Building, which housed the holding centre where I would be 'processed'.

To my surprise, there were about 50 other people from various countries at the centre. That was a relief. I was actually delighted at the thought of company instead of being locked up on my own. The others were from India, Africa, Pakistan and the West Indies, mostly men but a few women, some with children, who were placed in a separate section. There were a number of rooms in the facility and I was shown to one that I would share with six other men. There was not a single white person, while all the Securicor guards, male and female, were white. I remember thinking that this said a lot about UK immigration policy.

My delight at seeing so many other people in the centre was short lived: the sad faces there summed up the uncertainty that we all faced. I felt particularly sorry for the women and children, who were restricted to a small area where the children were not allowed to run around. An obese female Securicor officer shouted at the women whose children stepped out of line, telling them to 'keep your little bastards in order'. There were also racist remarks hurled at every opportunity and these would be received with heads bowed and in silence by people obviously hoping desperately not to antagonise and so, perhaps, win support for entry into the country.

After five days in that hell, where others had spent weeks and months, I was called out and told that my application for asylum had been refused and I would be returned to Belgium. I felt a sense of great relief as I was put on a flight to Brussels, and this time I was handed my documents and left from the departure lounge. I was so happy to get away that it was not until after the plane took off that I thought about the possible problems in re-entering Belgium. But I need not have worried; I was again stamped in and went to stay with Karl and Lyddy.

The routine continued as it had before until one morning in mid-May when neither Karl nor Lyddy was home. There was a knock at the door and when I opened it, there stood Omar and Maurice. We hugged and danced. They, too, had not been allowed into the UK and had also been put on a flight to Brussels. For the next few days we all squashed into the living room to sleep, but at the weekend the Becharts insisted we move to Mechelen, where they had spare rooms. They became 'Mum and Dad' to the three of us. At the same time, both Vilgot and Hussain sent us money to keep us going. Hussain had managed – how, we did not know at the time – to tap into some funding in the UK.

We helped with household chores and cooking and appointed Omar to manage our budget, which was supplemented by money earned when we were fortunate enough to get some part-time work with the International Confederation of Free Trade Unions in Brussels. We also made contact with human rights and support organisations in Belgium, which was particularly fortunate when I received news that my brother Joe was seriously ill in Lusaka – his heart defect had worsened and he required urgent surgery.

Although he worked for the ANC in Zambia while earning a living doing the accounts in a Lusaka business, when he fell ill his requests for help from the ANC were ignored. When I heard about this I asked Joe and his wife, Kamoo, to send me his medical records. As soon as I received the documents I made my way to Amsterdam, where Dutch anti-apartheid activists organised a fund to pay for Joe's operation and bring him, Kamoo and their two children to the Netherlands. They, too, had a terrible time at UK immigration before being allowed to continue with their journey. But they made it, thanks to the small group of Dutch activists. By that time, however, I also had problems: my Belgian visa would expire in September.

We were still in Mechelen and Omar and Maurice decided to accompany me to the aliens department in Brussels. We would all apply for extensions to stay in Belgium. Once again, the Belgians came up trumps. Although they interviewed us for several hours, they extended all our visas for another three months. I was ecstatic, but tragedy was about to strike. The Bechart family had invited Joe, who was scheduled to have his operation in the new year, and his family to Mechelen that December. They spent several pleasant days in the Belgian town and, when Mr Bechart was driving them back to

Amsterdam, there was an accident. Mr Bechart was killed, Joe was slightly injured and Kamoo and their two children escaped unhurt. I was devastated because 'Dad' Bechart was transporting my family.

Although 'Mum' Bechart kept assuring me that I should not feel guilty, that 'these things happen', even the news that some pressure was building in the UK to allow Maurice, Omar and me to go there failed to lift my spirits. Besides, I had heard all of this before. However, Hussain said that Martin Ennals of Amnesty International, supported by the Labour MP Joan Lestor, had made representations on our behalf to Merlyn Rees, Under Secretary of State in the Home Office. It was just as well I did not get my hopes up, because we were informed that entry had once again been refused and that it had been recommended that we be returned to Kenya.

This recommendation, based on our UNHCR status, changed our situation dramatically and we realised that we needed to move from Belgium to another country if we wanted to avoid going back to Africa. As a last-ditch effort, I wrote an appeal to the head of the Belgian police responsible for aliens, a Madame La Loux, asking her to grant us permanent refugee status in Belgium. To my complete surprise she instructed her officials to issue us with Belgian UN refugee documents, which invalidated the documents issued in Kenya. Our place of residence, in UN terms, was now Belgium.

The Belgian documents, we were sure, would make our entry into the UK much easier. But this time we would not fly and therefore would not arrive at either Gatwick or Heathrow. We would go by sea, sailing from the Hoek of Holland. As it had been when we started out from South Africa all those years ago, it was just Omar and me. Maurice, by that time, had become romantically involved with a Belgian woman and said he might follow us later if we succeeded in our venture.

It had been a year since I had last been through the ritual of trying to enter the UK. As usual, we were unsettled throughout the voyage. I kept asking myself why I was once again placing myself in a position to be humiliated at the hands of some bigoted official. Could it really be worth it to again be escorted through the baggage hall to collect my bags and through the public areas as people stared? I started to pray, while, at the same time, vowing that this would definitely be my last attempt to get into the UK. I would go to whatever alternative was offered. At least, I consoled myself, I was not seasick and, anyway, racism existed everywhere.

As the ferry approached Harwich, Omar and I stood nervously on the deck, and I remember that when we disembarked my heart was pounding and I was praying under my breath, while trying to appear relaxed. I tried to picture what my facial expression projected, trying to relax muscles that I was sure would give my nervousness away; I had to appear normal. The queue to the immigration counters seemed to move very slowly, but suddenly it was my turn. I handed over my papers, trying hard to stop my hand shaking.

I was almost afraid to look up, but the man behind the counter smiled, wished me 'Good morning', flicked through the papers, stamped them and waved me on. I had 'leave to enter the UK for three months'. Omar had the same experience.

We could not believe what had happened. It must be the prayers, I thought, but as we walked toward the train station we both worried that, at any moment, we would be stopped and told that there had been a mistake. Hussain had instructed me to catch a train to Victoria and call him. By midday we were in the one-bedroom flat in Clapham Junction that he shared with Myra. It was smiles all round. We had our accommodation, sleeping in the lounge until further notice. We had made it at last.

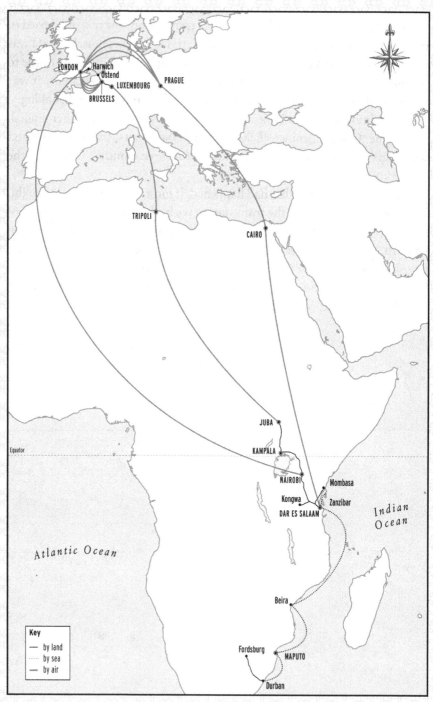

Amin's journey

CHAPTER 23

Coming to terms with exile

In the weeks following our arrival in London Martin Ennals put us in touch with Joan Lestor, who advised us to apply for admission to a college and for student visas. Although it was April and the academic year only started in September or October, everything fell into place. Wandsworth Technical College, around the corner from Hussain's flat, accepted us for the last term of the academic year to start a two-year course to do A levels in economics and sociology. At that time college fees were minimal and Hussain had managed to secure documents showing that we had sufficient financial support to apply for and obtain student visas. Hussain, who had already secured residency by marrying a British national, joined us at the college.

Maurice then arrived. All three of us were having to rely on Hussain, who simply said it was fine and we should not worry, but gave no explanation. We decided we could no longer do this; that we should appeal to the International Defence and Aid Fund (IDAF), established by the British anti-apartheid cleric Canon John Collins and staffed mainly by exiled members of the SACP. IDAF, we knew, provided funding for legal aid in South African political trials and assisted exiles and refugees. We also knew by then that a number of well-known people in the movement had been generously helped by the fund. As we saw it, without Hussain, we three would be penniless, homeless and our chances of remaining in the UK would be jeopardised.

So we went to the IDAF headquarters in Islington and were directed to the office of a well-known member of the COD and the SACP, Phyllis Altman. She greeted us and we explained our situation: that we were in need of assistance to tide us over until we could find our feet. She listened without showing any emotion and never asked any questions. She then reached into a drawer, took out three half-crown (two shillings and sixpence – 25p) coins and slid them across the desk to us. We just stared and then walked out, leaving the coins on the desk.

IDAF, we decided, was a 'closed shop' where a few individuals decided who would be helped and how. Maurice was so disgusted with the reception we had received that he decided to write a critical document about the ANC and our experiences in Kongwa. This would highlight what was wrong with the movement. His aim was to distribute it to a limited number of exiles in London to show how far the movement had drifted from the ideals we once thought it stood for.

But when I told Hussain what had happened, he confided that he had penetrated the barrier set up at IDAF by mainly SACP personnel and had become a close confidant of Canon Collins, with whom he had regular meetings. Through Collins he had arranged for us to receive allowances until we were able to secure other sources of income through scholarships or employment. That was where the funding had been coming from.

Maurice completed his critical document. By then there were a number of prominent South Africans in London who had become disillusioned with the ANC. Some, like Barney Desai, George Peake and Lionel Morrison, had joined the PAC, which we thought was a mistake. We felt we should all unite and help to get the movement on the right track. For this reason we visited George Peake and showed him the document. He asked us to leave it with him so he could read through it and return it later. We agreed, and soon regretted how naive we had been because not much later the critique was published.

An edited version appeared in the South African *Sunday Times* and the document also surfaced in *Black Dwarf* magazine, edited by the British radical Tariq 'Ali'. There were political differences within the group who published *Black Dwarf*, and the decision to publish Maurice's document apparently brought these to the surface, resulting in a split and the emergence of another magazine, *Red Dwarf*.

We were furious, since we considered that such publicity about the problems of the anti-apartheid movement in exile merely helped the enemy. It could also, we realised, be seen by PAC members as a way of boosting their organisation. Fingers were pointed at who might be responsible and these were followed by denials, but it did not matter who had put the document out, the damage was done.

However, by that time we were secure, having obtained funding for our studies and having exchanged our Belgian documents for British papers. We also had good relationships with our economics and sociology lecturers, who were sympathetic to the South African struggle and allowed us time off whenever we needed it. This 'off time' usually involved our ongoing concern about comrades who were still stuck in Kenya or other African countries. Tjitte de Fries in Holland had set up an organisation, Stichting ISARA, to assist South African refugees and I liaised with him from London.

One of the comrades I communicated with was 'Mogorosi', who had left the ANC in Zambia but was free to move around Lusaka. It seemed that the movement no longer tried to enforce its will on comrades who were determined not to be bullied. Gerald was also free to move around and we heard he had secured employment in Lusaka. But 'Mogorosi' was having difficulties and wanted to study. With help, he could get to the UK, which was, at that time, providing British colonial passports to citizens fleeing Rhodesia. So 'Mogorosi' declared himself to be Rhodesian and gained entry after Hussain had arranged his fare, presumably through Canon Collins.

By the time 'Mogorosi' arrived Omar had found employment and moved out. An anti-apartheid American fellow student, John Childers, and I had moved to a one-room apartment I had found. There 'Mogorosi' joined us and, with John contributing to my scholarship income, we were able to survive while 'Mogorosi' tried to find a place at a university and funding for his studies. He was also able to brief us on the then current situation in Lusaka.

He told us that after the disastrous incursions into Rhodesia – known as the Wankie and Sipolilo campaigns – the army was demoralised and depleted and the struggle had come to a standstill. There had been serious recriminations, claims and counterclaims had been made, there were divisions, and conferences and meetings were held. The blame game came into play. Some of the comrades, among them Joe Cotton, were sent to Eastern Europe on scholarships.

After what 'Mogorosi' had told us, we were even more wary of meeting any ANC officials. But a few months after his arrival, Hussain and I unavoidably met Zola Zembe and Reg September, who were among the most senior ANC and SACP people in London. We were walking down Tottenham Court Road when we saw the two approaching us. Unsure of how to react, we paused and then, to our surprise, Zola walked straight up and embraced us. He turned to Reg, announced us as comrades, and said something about our bond from Kongwa not being able to be broken. We were taken aback, exchanged pleasantries and moved on. Nothing was asked of us and we never saw them again.

In 1971 Omar, Hussain and I sat for our A level exams. While we were waiting for the results (we all passed) Omar tried unsuccessfully to obtain a grant so that he could continue to study accountancy. Through links I had established I was advised to contact the Student Christian Movement of

LEFT: *Amin Cajee*

RIGHT: *Pat Cajee, formerly Pat Shanks. She and Amin married in 1972. They met after Amin approached Pat, as assistant general secretary of the Student Christian Movement of Great Britain and Ireland, for help with getting a grant for Omar from the Africa Education Trust.*

Great Britain and Ireland and to ask for Pat Shanks, assistant general secretary of the organisation. She had close links with Pat Herbert, the head of the Africa Education Trust, which supported exile students from Southern Africa. Zambia's then president, Kenneth Kaunda, was once a grant recipient.

Omar had suffered earlier rejections and when I forwarded this information to him he asked if I could go on his behalf to explore the possibility. With some reluctance I arranged a meeting with Pat Shanks. She was extremely helpful and immediately phoned the Africa Education Trust and explained Omar's situation. The grant was approved. Pat was obviously someone who could be of great help in any future applications for refugees. So, both for this reason and to thank her for her efforts for Omar, I invited her out to lunch and, fortunately, found I had enough money to pay for it.

I was right about Pat being able to help and this was the first of many meetings. During one she introduced me to Dr Wilson Conco, a former Treason Trialist, who was a trustee of the Lutuli Memorial Foundation. As a result, I spent several months doing administrative work at the foundation before finding employment in the accounts department of the Inner London Education Authority (ILEA). Pat and I continued to see one another, I started courting her and, on 16 September 1972, we were married.

The extended Cajee family in London, 2016: First row sitting Daulah, Yahya, Zaqiya, Eesa behind. Back row Baby Uthmaan, holding him Nasir, Mazbin, Amin, Pat, Gayle (Hannah), Zamir.

Almost from the week that I met her, Pat and I were involved in helping other comrades who were stranded. This was often made possible by the Student Christian Movement and even the Irish government. Alfred Shabangu and a PAC couple, David and Miriam Ratladi, for example, had met in Nairobi and managed, somehow, to get to Italy. There they were housed in a refugee camp in Trieste, where, to their horror, they discovered refugees from World War II still living. They were desperate, but Alfred managed to contact me and I suggested they get into Holland. Once in the Netherlands they should apply for refugee papers and stay in contact.

This was much the way these things operated. Once the three of them got to Amsterdam, where we had contacts, Pat, through the Student Christian Movement, tried to get the UK to accept them, but this proved impossible. The Irish government came to the rescue and provided papers, but the local Anti-Apartheid Movement, headed by ANC- and SACP-aligned individuals, refused assistance. David and Miriam eventually moved to the UK from Ireland, while Alfred went back to Holland.

It was a time when all our circumstances were changing: 'Mogorosi' had received a scholarship to Edinburgh, Maurice decided to return to Belgium, Pat and I started married life in a flat in Baron's Court, and Omar moved on to study accountancy. I had to inform the Home Office that I had married and, in early 1973, received another dose of racism. One day the neighbours informed us that a policewoman had been around enquiring about us and asking very personal questions, such as were we living together? Did I come home regularly or occasionally? This was obviously a Home Office check to ensure that ours was not a marriage of convenience. That I understood.

But the very next evening the policewoman reappeared at our door unannounced to interview me and Pat in a way that shocked us both. Most of the questions were directed to Pat. It was as if I was not in the room. Was Pat happy and did I treat her well? How come she was earning more than me? She then warned Pat that she should be careful because 'some of these people' could not be trusted. I was boiling with anger, but felt I had to keep cool and composed. The interview lasted an hour and after she left I remember that Pat rushed to the toilet and was sick.

I continued working with the ILEA, on the fourth floor of Queensborough House, going in to work each day completely unaware that two floors up was another of our Kongwa escapees. I only discovered this in 1976 when I was walking in Brixton one Saturday and literally bumped into a man on the crowded street. We both looked up, stared and then hugged one another as we danced. It was 'Van'. We were both in a hurry, so he gave me his address in Brixton and we arranged to meet there that evening.

Pat was then pregnant with our first son, Zamir, whose arrival, and that of his brother, Nasir, two years later, would joyously change our lives forever. We made our way to the address 'Van' had given us, expecting to see Doreen, but we were greeted by 'Van' and his new wife, Jabu, who was also pregnant. During our chat he told me that, just as he had decided to follow Omar, 'Ali' and me to Nairobi, he had decided to follow us to London. With no way of contacting any of us, he had found a job with the ILEA. Using his full name, he worked in Queensborough House, on the sixth floor.

So, for two years we had worked in the same building and our paths had never crossed. He also told me that he and Doreen had parted, but he was able to give me her address. She and the Makubus became part of a growing social circle of exiles who came and went and included those who still remained part of the ANC.

The difference was that those still 'with the movement' never made any mention of my past and did not ask about Kongwa or my experiences. Even Dr Dadoo (Mota), with whom I often went to lunch, did not talk or ask about what had happened. I think he was just pleased that I had come out of everything alive. I was also received warmly by comrades I had known in Fordsburg and who had spent more than a decade in UK exile. Some, such as Aziz Pahad and Issy Dinath, went on to become major players in national and local government after the 1994 transition.

Charlie and Harlene Jassat also relocated from Dar es Salaam to London and it was in their home in 1994 that I again met Joe Modise. I was invited for lunch and, when I walked in, I saw Joe seated at the table. It was shortly before he became Minister of Defence in Nelson Mandela's government. I felt good. Here was positive proof that the ANC could not reach me. So I sat down and, once again, there was no mention of my past. I recall that Joe spent most of the meal discussing the food, probably to avoid any other topics. But he addressed me as 'comrade' as he left and said: 'We have achieved political freedom, but we will never achieve economic freedom.'

This sort of general discussion about the situation in South Africa was the norm in all those years and the only comrades who ever enquired about how I came to be in London and what had happened in Kongwa were known 'dissidents' such as George Peake. Apart from times when I met with comrades with whom I had shared experiences, there were never any questions about why, how and when I had left for exile. I was simply a comrade who happened to be in London.

In 1983 I joined the Ethnic Minorities Unit set up by the Greater London Council under Ken Livingstone and headed by Herman Ouseley, later to become Baron Ouseley, and his deputy, Ansel Wong. I felt I was again joining the war that I had started fighting in Fordsburg all those years ago, only using different tactics in a different theatre of action. The right-wing media hounded Livingstone, labelling him 'Red Ken', ridiculing his policies and, in particular, those supportive of women, gays, lesbians and ethnic minorities. In my Ethnic Minorities Unit capacity I not only worked on grant reports and organised conferences and cultural events, I proudly played a role in the successful London against Racism campaign in 1984.

The highlight of that time was launching the acclaimed Anne Frank exhibition in London with Jan Erik Dubbelman of the Anne Frank Foundation in Holland. This exhibition was the start of what became a series of global educational programmes to promote human rights and to combat bigotry and discrimination.

It was a wonderful period, but, after the arrival of Margaret Thatcher's Conservative government, the Greater London Council was closed down. However, I managed to find a post heading a team dealing with 'migrants, travellers and the Irish community' that was set up by Camden Council's London Strategic Policy Unit.

It was here that I saw how racism can function in various, perhaps unexpected, ways and learned a lesson about why it is always best, certainly in such situations, to be transparent. The lesson concerned 'Mogorosi', by then known as Michael Thomolang. He had completed his studies in Edinburgh and had returned to London to look for a job, when a number of posts came up in my section.

I advised him to apply, even though I usually chaired the selection panel of three. There were seven candidates for this particular post and 'Mogorosi' was the only African. I stepped down as chair, but did not let on that we knew one another, because I knew – as did 'Mogorosi' – that he was not the best qualified candidate and that I would have to vote against his appointment. One should not expect prejudice in the sort of section we were working in, but there was prejudice. The better candidates were of European and Asian origin, but, by two votes to my one against, 'Mogorosi' got the job.

I was his line manager and responsible for his training, so we continued to pretend not to know one another. Then, a month later, this pretence exploded in our faces when I had to take my two sons to work with me. We were very close as a family and they had met all our friends and were fond of 'Uncle Mogorosi'. He had stayed with us and had, at one stage, regularly driven them to school.

'Mogorosi' happened to be in the office as we entered and was the first person the boys saw. They promptly rushed towards him shouting, 'Uncle "Mogorosi"!' They hugged him, as the rest of the staff looked on. I was deeply embarrassed, knowing that nepotism would be suspected. It was. The interview files were examined, but they revealed that I had selected another candidate and had objected to appointing 'Mogorosi', so there the matter rested.

In any event, it turned out well because, having been given the opportunity to prove himself, 'Mogorosi' became a valuable member of my team. He later moved to the housing department in London's Islington Council. The frontline service skills he acquired seemed to serve him well when he later moved back to post-apartheid South Africa to work in the home affairs department.

Throughout this time, there were regular discussions with other exiles and news would continue to filter through about what was happening, both in South Africa and among the exiled comrades. In some ways, I think, we were better informed than many of those within the ANC. There was a classic example in the early post-apartheid years, after I had become head of the information and advice service of the Lewisham Council in South East London. I established a link between the Lewisham Council and its counterpart in Ekurhuleni, east of Johannesburg, and notified the new South African High Commission of this fact. The response was that no such place existed and that there was no such word in any of the local languages. But we finally got that straightened out.

I had been appointed to the Lewisham post in 1988. It involved providing a comprehensive range of services to residents, including library-based video links and 'one-stop' services centres. But South Africa remained an abiding focus and, by the mid-1990s, with the support of council and the local library service, we teamed up with former Rivonia Trialist Denis Goldberg in a project that shipped a mobile library and hundreds of thousands of books to South Africa. I felt I was doing something worthwhile, not only for myself and my family, but for the cause of non-racialism that had been central to our South African struggle.

Some of the information that came through from old comrades also made me feel that I had taken the right decision to flee to Kenya and avoid the Wankie adventure. A good example was when Doreen rang me one day and asked me to come over as she had a surprise for me. I rushed over and when I walked through the door there was Thula, one of the Operation 29 accused. We embraced and he told me he had received a scholarship to study in the Netherlands. Over a long afternoon he related his experiences after leaving Kongwa and going to 'the front', where, he said, the comrades were not given 'enough supplies for even one battle'.

Thula was captured in 1967 with a number of other comrades during the Wankie fiasco and was held on death row in the Rhodesian capital, Salisbury (now Harare). Over the next ten and more years, he and the others were occasionally marched to what he called the 'execution cell' next to the gallows, only to be marched back again the next day. He was also interrogated by South African security men and was shocked when they produced files containing photographs of comrades in Kongwa.

For more than a decade he waited to die within hours, but, during the talks about an independent Zimbabwe, all executions were suspended. When Rhodesia finally became Zimbabwe in April 1980, Thula and his comrades thought freedom had finally come. A year later, they were still in prison, still on what had been death row and had no outside contacts.

They were finally able to get a letter to a lawyer who was visiting a client in the prison and explained their predicament to him. The lawyer managed to inform President Robert Mugabe's office that a number of South African guerrilla fighters were still being held in prison. Mugabe immediately instructed that they be released. Thula said that he and the other prisoners had felt that they were being held at the request of the ANC and that since Joshua Nkomo, the head of ZAPU and a close ally of the ANC, was the Home Minister he had complied. The ANC, he thought, feared their release would trigger a negative vision of the Wankie escapade and add to the problems already evident within the army, by then based mainly in Angola.

Looking at what had happened over the years and talking with comrades such as Thula caused me to question whether we had ever really had an armed struggle in South Africa. With the exception of a number of sabotage acts spread over many years, there was no full-scale confrontation between the apartheid forces and our fighters. The country in general was peaceful when compared, for example, to Northern Ireland.

It was only when the courageous students of Soweto began what was a largely spontaneous uprising in 1976 that we saw anything of the military might of the apartheid state used against the people. But it was a people who were neither well equipped nor trained, and their rising against a formidable enemy should not be credited to any established organisation. I think that part of the reason it came about was the absence of the long-awaited and long-promised armed struggle. Sitting in London and recruiting people to fly into South Africa to bring in banned literature while attending international conferences and meetings does not constitute an armed struggle. These actions posed no real threat to the government.

Yet there was an armed struggle away from the borders of South Africa and, sadly, within MK. Comrades perished unnecessarily as a result of a dubious military strategy. While young Sowetans and other young people in various parts of the country clambered to recreate the armed struggle, instead of moving the struggle closer to home, the leadership moved it further north, to Angola. There our comrades were involved in a civil war, while most wanted to go home to fight. So the mistakes of Kongwa were repeated, with more disastrous and often deadly consequences. In 1984, there was a mutiny and comrades died. Then there was a brutal crackdown and the later reports of deaths and torture in the prison camps. As a result, I feel grateful that the Tanzanian government had the foresight to withhold arms from the ANC in Kongwa.

As I look back across the years, two issues in particular continue to concern me: the negotiated settlement between the apartheid government and the ANC and the question of my deserting MK. I now think that because of the level of penetration of MK and the ANC by the apartheid security apparatus, the negotiated settlement was probably inevitable. It brought together a corrupt political elite in the country with an infiltrated exile movement that also contained much corruption. Yet this quite dramatic change did not come about because of an armed struggle. The parties were forced into a deal by the uprisings of the youth, the emergence of militant internal trade unions, the state of the apartheid economy and the resultant pressure from business and the international community.

As to being accused in some quarters of being a 'deserter', I acknowledge that this might be appropriate. But I do not accept it when it comes from those who kept themselves away in the countries of Europe, gaining one academic qualification after another and complaining that their substantial stipends were inadequate. Nor from those who enjoyed lives of comfort, acquired property and returned to South Africa with bulging pockets to move into gentrified neighbourhoods and positions of power.

I volunteered to serve what I saw as a democratic movement dedicated to bringing down an oppressive and racist regime. Instead, I found myself serving a movement that was relentless in exercising power and riddled with corruption. I had to take a decision to continue being party to this or to exit. I chose to exit.

I do accept criticism of my choice from those few of my comrades who survived the tragedies of Wankie, Angola and elsewhere. If I bow my head it is to those who understood the military futility, but who decided it was better to die fighting than to flee. I took the path of flight because I thought I could make a better contribution to the wider struggle by living. That was my decision and I am happy to live with it.

Afterword

I have my own experiences within the Congress movement, over a similar period to that of Amin Cajee, although in different theatres. But this is Amin's story – one that I have tried for many years to get him to tell. Over those times of talking, interviewing and emailing, Amin finally agreed to tell of his journey from Fordsburg as one of probably the first two 'Indians' recruited from within the country to join South Africa's 'armed struggle'. He saw this as primarily a record for his grandchildren. I see it as so much more.

In the process of putting the preceding chapters together, trying at all times to reflect Amin's voice and views in his own words, I became more acutely aware of the circumstances and the pressures that applied to those early volunteers to Umkhonto we Sizwe (MK). It gave me a clearer understanding of how events unfolded and how that legacy is still felt in the South Africa of today.

Although every effort was made to try to establish what had happened to those individuals whose names – often along with various MK pseudonyms – feature prominently in Amin's story, this sometimes proved impossible. Even in the official ANC list of those killed in the incursions into Rhodesia the identity of some who died is clearly unknown.

Many of the MK volunteers were young, in their teens and early twenties, most with little experience of the world outside of their rural villages or urban townships. A few, such as 21-year-old Chris Hani, were well educated; they were quickly absorbed into the ranks of the SACP and catapulted into leadership roles. Among a core of idealists of one kind or another there were also drunkards, thieves, and opportunists; in fact, a goodly cross-section of the legislated underclass of the brutal apartheid system.

The leadership of this movement decreed that the ANC was the sole legitimate representative of 'the people of South Africa'. It was 'mother and father' to those who joined and any dissent was in opposition to the will of the people, treasonous in fact. Such simplistic slogans had the effect of giving unmitigated authority to those put in charge and who could, with impunity, impose arbitrary punishments. However, they also served to maintain broad unity within a potentially fractious exile community.

And unity was the priority for the ANC's acting president, OR Tambo. It was his great achievement to be able to hold together such a disparate group in an atmosphere of fear, factionalism and paranoia. He fostered and, when need be, enforced a culture of consensus. This he was able to do only by turning a blind eye to many abuses and by being prepared, when rebellion threatened, to send in what he called 'the big stick'.

In the politically bipolar world of the 1960s, the West – epitomised by the United States – opposed any insurrections in Southern Africa. Portugal was still the colonial master of Angola and Mozambique and a member of the NATO military alliance, Britain still had nominal charge of Southern Rhodesia (Zimbabwe) and there existed strong military and economic ties with the apartheid state that still controlled South West Africa (Namibia). So it was to the East, to the Soviet bloc and to China that would-be liberation movements turned for support.

However, by 1961 this proclaimed socialist fifth of the world was in a state of flux: tensions between the Soviet Union and China were soon to result in a schism that would have profound repercussions in communist parties and liberation movements everywhere. But in the early years before what is now referred to as the Sino-Soviet split, some MK recruits went for military training in China, where an aggressive stance towards the West was developing. As the Chinese government saw it, the colonies of Southern Africa, along with apartheid South Africa, were new centres of revolution.

But the Soviet Union was developing a policy of peaceful co-existence with the West that did not preclude assistance to existing national liberation movements. The argument was that the capitalist West was in a state of decay; that the Soviet bloc would, within 20 years, have the highest standard of living in the world and, as veteran ANC and former MK member Ronnie Kasrils has noted, 'the decisive victory would be won in the battle against capitalism'.

It now seems obvious that this frankly unrealistic view led to an assessment that pro-Soviet forces in Angola, Mozambique and Zimbabwe would eventually dominate. MK, with these allies, would then be able to dislodge the apartheid government in a conventional military confrontation. This resulted in all but the earliest MK volunteers being trained only in conventional warfare, from managing tanks and artillery to anti-aircraft batteries. Soviet foreign policy, therefore, helped to strangle any real prospect of a popular guerrilla movement emerging in South Africa.

This approach was also reinforced by a dogmatic view within the SACP that apartheid South Africa was a 'fascist state'. As such, it was decreed that no legitimate trade union or workers' movement could develop in the country; it would either be subsumed by the state or crushed. As with fascism in Europe, it would have to be overcome by an army coming in from beyond the borders.

This tactical and ideological confusion was manifest in the military camps in Tanzania and Zambia when volunteers returned from training. A number of them, including Amin Cajee and Pat Molaoa, saw the option of a 'liberation army' sweeping into South Africa from outside as romantic nonsense. It was this, as much as the frustration of being stuck for months and years in camps far from home, that led to a rebellion in Kongwa in 1966. These factors, as well as being drafted in to fight on one side in a civil war, led to the much more serious mutiny in Angola 18 years later.

These issues, particularly in the early years, were exacerbated by the fact that the ANC was only one member, although the leader, of an ethnically based alliance. Only in April 1969 could members of 'other nationalities' join the ANC. And it was only in 1985 that members of 'other groups' could serve on the executive of an alliance that comprised the ANC, the Indian congresses, the Coloured People's Congress and the COD (for those classified 'white'). Compounding this problem was the linguistically based animosity among isiZulu, isiXhosa and Sesotho/Setswana speakers that had been encouraged by apartheid.

Added to this volatile mix was corruption at various levels, evidence of nepotism and the exercise of often brutal authority. These charges, amounting to what was referred to as the 'rot' in the ANC, came strongly to the fore in 1969 when they were advanced in a memorandum signed by Chris Hani and six MK comrades. They had survived the incursions into Zimbabwe that saw Rhodesian and South African forces defeated in two firefights, providing a considerable propaganda boost for the ANC. However, as Tambo later commented, the ventures across the Zambezi amounted to 'an heroic failure'.

What Amin and most of the recruits in Kongwa were unaware of was that their youthful camp commissar, Chris Hani, had argued with the leadership that it might be possible to establish a 'bridge' – a series of supply points – through Zimbabwe to allow for infiltration into South Africa. This thinking was modelled on the Ho Chi Minh trail from north to south through the jungles of Vietnam. So it was Hani who commanded the main Luthuli Detachment, together with elements of the Soviet-supported ZIPRA, the armed wing of ZAPU. Only eight of the original 100 members of the detachment managed to escape to Botswana, where they were jailed for 18 months.

On their return Hani and his comrades distributed their memorandum and, in an ironic twist, were accused of treason and sentenced to death. This sentence was subsequently overturned by Tambo and, at the Morogoro conference in 1969, tensions within MK were defused by a degree of open consultation and promises of reform. Hani, who had relocated on his own to the Zambian Copperbelt, was persuaded to rejoin the ANC and MK. He clearly thought he could do more within the movement than outside, accepting that much within it was still 'rotten'.

However, similar conditions continued and, in some reported cases, became worse. The scale of abuses, of extrajudicial executions and torture in the camps of MK, especially after they were relocated to Angola after 1974, increased. All in the cause of maintaining unity in the name of the people of South Africa. But there were also many examples of heroism and nobility in conditions that were often horrendous. And, after the 1976 student uprising in South Africa, there were also many more volunteers as youthful as the first Kongwa contingent. The same frustrations applied, compounded by this army being thrown into battle against one side in the Angolan civil war.

When this exploded into mutiny the reaction by the leadership was harsh. It led, as an internal ANC report noted, to 'staggering brutality, extraordinary abuse of power'. Some details of this were spelled out in the 2015 book *If We Must Die* by former MK commander Stanley Manong.

This, then, is part of the South African legacy and needs to be confronted, discussed and debated. To date, there have been a few exposés, especially of the events in Angola in the 1980s, but, as far as I am aware, Amin Cajee's story is the first detailed account of life in Kongwa camp, the 1966 'mutiny' and its aftermath. The flight of Amin and other exiles from an exiled movement and their attempts to gain sanctuary in Europe also has echoes of the enormously greater refugee tragedy that began playing out along the Mediterranean coast in 2015. As such, the story of this young Fordsburg fighter and his comrades carries lessons that I think we all ignore at our peril.

Terry Bell
Cape Town, 2016

MK deaths in Zimbabwe incursions 1967/68
(Official ANC list)

February, Basil (Paul Peterson)
Makgotsi, Jones
Mampuru, Christopher
Maseko, Don Donga
Masemeni, James
Mhlongo, John
Modumo, Ernest (Steven
   Maelebyane)
Motsepe, Andries
Sharp, Alfred
Sibanyoni, Delmas
Baloi, Robert
Masipa, Barry
Moloi, Sparks
Setsoba, Charles (Jack Simelane)
Donda (from Natal)
Mahamba, Sparks
Mhambi, Charles (Rhodes Msuntu
   Ngamela)
Nduna, Eric
Donga
Mbali, Jackson
Ndlovu, Joseph Spoe
Nduku, Knox

Nondulo, Ernest
Theo, Mkhaliphi
Bandon, Gordan
Basset, Basel (Jampie Brooklane)
Biyela, Philimon
Goniwe, Jacques
Hlatswayo, Hlatswayo
Hlekani, Gandi
Joseph, Zami
Maloma, Tony
Mayona, Sydwell
Melani, Lenon
Mkhaba, William
Mkhonza, Zelan
Mgwacela, Badman
Molefe, David (Phoko)
Mosedi, Patrick (Molowa)
Mthusi, George
Mzati, Kenneth
Ngalo, Ben
Poo, Mike (Festus Nturu
   Boikhutso)
Tsele, Benson
Tsotetsi, Stanley

Major figures in a seven-year odyssey

The recruiters

Paul Joseph: born 1930, factory worker and trade unionist who was an executive member of both the Transvaal Indian Congress and the SACP. Accused in the 1956 Treason Trial, he was one of the earliest members of and recruiter for MK. Retired and lives in London.

Suliman 'Babla' Saloojee: born 1931. A legal clerk and political activist in Fordsburg responsible for smuggling activists out of the country and helping produce underground literature. Banned, detained and tortured. Killed 1964 after 'falling' from seventh floor window of security police HQ.

Kongwa camp, Tanzania, comrades accused of treason

Patrick Modise/Mosidi/Molaoa: born 1925, high school graduate, boxer, ANC Youth League national president, 'first string' accused in 1956 Treason Trial in South Africa. Volunteered for MK training and was sent to China. Killed in the 1967/68 incursions into Southern Rhodesia, received posthumous Order of Luthuli in gold, 2003.

Mntungwa (Vincent Khumalo): senior ANC branch official in the 1950s. As Ken Mntungwa, became ANC acting chief representative in Lusaka in 1970 and chief representative in Dar es Salaam. Returned to Lusaka in 1973 as a isiZulu-language broadcaster on Radio Freedom. Died in car accident 1974.

Amin Kajee (Cajee): born 1942, raised mainly in Fordsburg, recruited into MK in 1962 by Paul Joseph. One of the two 'Indians' first sent abroad for military training. Trained in Czechoslovakia. Fled to Nairobi from Dar es Salaam 1967. Father of two sons and with five grandchildren, retired and lives with wife, Pat, in London.

The others trained in Czechoslovakia

Omar Moosa (Bhamjee): born in Fordsburg, 1940. Recruited into MK with Amin Cajee. Escaped from Kongwa camp, Tanzania, 1967. Bookkeeper/accountant, died in Leicester, England, 2000.

Ali (Hussain Jacobs): born in Pretoria. Recruited to MK in 1963 by Babla Saloojee and sent abroad for military training in Czechoslovakia. Left Dar es Salaam for Nairobi in 1967 with Amin Cajee. Married with three sons and a daughter. In 2016 a very successful entrepreneur based in London.

Zee/Zelani Mkhonzo: born about 1942. Recruited in Johannesburg, communications specialist. Killed in Rhodesia incursions. Nothing more is currently available.

Gerald Lockman (Sisulu): born 1944, nephew of anti-apartheid icons Walter and Albertina Sisulu, who adopted him, aged eight months. Fled into exile aged 19, joined MK, described plans to infiltrate South Africa via military incursions into Southern Rhodesia as 'suicidal', deserted and escaped to Zambia. Married, set up business on the Zambian Copperbelt. Died in Kitwe in 2010.

Joseph Cotton (Kotane): born in Cape Town in 1940, son of Communist Party leader Moses Kotane and his first wife. Named after Joseph Stalin. Took on the 'exile name' Cotton apparently to avoid being linked to his father who was both the general secretary of the SACP and treasurer-general of the ANC. South African ambassador to Algeria in 2012. In 2016 apparently retired and living in Centurion, Gauteng, South Africa.

George Driver (James April): born in Cape Town, 1940. University graduate, student teacher. Arrested in 1962 with Basil February for slogan painting. Helped by Babla Saloojee to escape to Botswana in 1963. Involved in firefight on banks of Zambezi during incursions. Infiltrated South Africa, 1970. Arrested, served 15 years on Robben Island. Died 2016.

Paul Peterson (Basil February): born in Cape Town, 1944. Medical student, arrested with James April, and left the country with him. Involved in fierce firefights in Rhodesia, 1967. Separated from comrades, reportedly hijacked a car to continue south. Killed by security forces.

Stanley (Abdul Satar Tayob): Volunteered for MK apparently to escape an arranged marriage. Returned to South Africa via India after military training and handed himself over to police. In 2016 a shopkeeper in Gauteng.

Bobby (Amin Cajee): Volunteered for MK to join his friend Stanley 'for the adventure'. Surrendered to police on return to South Africa. Contacted Amin Cajee more than 20 years later to apologise. Died of a heart attack in Durban circa 2010.

The third recruit

Magan Narsee Chhiba: born in Fordsburg 1948. Stayed behind because of family commitments when Amin Cajee and Omar Bhamjee left for military training. Later, with Amin's older brother Joe and Nanoo Jasmath, bombed the 11th Street post office. An artist, signwriter and calligrapher, died of a heart attack in 2002. Posthumously declared a Human Rights Champion by the Lenasia Human Rights Association.

Acknowledgements

In the first place, there is my mother and my sisters, who endured years of police harassment because of me. And my brother Yussuf – 'Joe' – who first made me politically aware, as well as my nephews and nieces who continued to extend their warm support. Particular mention must be made of Hussain – 'Ali' – Jacobs, and the late Omar Bhamjee and to all those fallen comrades, including Zee, 'Pat', Mogorosi, 'Boetie', Gerald and Ahmed, along with those with whom I had differences and those who have survived to this date. It was an honour to be associated with you in the struggle.

My thanks must go to Major Chikombele of Tanzania and there is special appreciation and thanks, as well as heartfelt apologies, to the Harman family of Kongwa who provided us with many meals, and who lost their livelihood and were deported from Tanzania for being associated with us.

Harlene and Abdulhay – 'Charlie' – Jassat's hospitality at a difficult time made life easier for us in Dar es Salaam, as did the material and moral support given us in Nairobi by Banu and his wife, Prakash, along with the Rauf Khan family.

I often wonder how we might have coped in Belgium had it not been for 'Mom and Dad' Becart and their son and daughter, Karl and Lyddy, and for the help in Europe extended by the late Tjitte de Fries and Artie and Fritz Hoogenhout in Amsterdam.

Over more than 40 years in London, the support, encouragement and help received in the Greater London Council Ethnic Minority and Strategic Policy units and by Ansel Wong, Kenny Williamson, Tariq Hafeez, and later, the Lewisham Council, remains memorable. From councillors such as Pauline Morrisson, Mee Ling and Jimmy Aderfiryane to Lewisham chief executives Terry Hanifin and Barry Quirk, along with Julia Newton and the information team (they know who they are), I thank you all.

I also want to thank the Qureshi family and Dalpat Lala for their warm friendship and support.

Over the years, many people have encouraged me to write, including Paul Joseph, Denis Goldberg, Tariq Hafeez and Kenny Williamson. But this book would not have appeared without the encouragement and hard work of Terry and Barbara Bell. And it also owes much to the fact that my wife Pat has stayed by my side for the past 44 years. Thank you, Pat.

Notes

1 The Treason Trial was a trial in which 156 people, including Nelson Mandela, were arrested in a raid in 1956 and accused of treason. The main trial lasted until 1961, when all the defendants were found not guilty.

2 In 1962 the South African government published a list of 'persons who have been office-bearers, officers, members or active supporters of the Communist Party of South Africa'. Harmel was a member of the Central Committee of the Communist Party and its foremost theoretician, as well as a member of the High Command of Umkhonto we Sizwe.

3 The staff included Alfred Hutchinson, Joan Anderson, Disa Putini, Dan Tloome, Moosa Moosajee, Herby Pillay and Mervyn Thandary.

4 On March 21 in Sharpeville township, South African police fired on a peaceful demonstration against the pass laws, killing 69 people, most of them shot in the back while fleeing.

5 The Immorality Act prohibited sex between whites and blacks.

6 In July 1963 the high command of MK was arrested at Liliesleaf Farm in the Johannesburg suburb of Rivonia and subsequently sentenced to life imprisonment.

7 Nokwe.

Printed in the United States
By Bookmasters